Life on Turkeyneck Hill

A Memoir

PHYLLIS DOW BEX

FORWARD BY STEPHEN CRANE

Name: Phyllis Dow Bex
Title: Life on Turkeyneck Hill: A Memoir
Identifiers: LCCN: 2024903881
ISBN: 9798989685226 (paperback)
      9798989685240 (hard cover)
      9798989685233 (e-book)

Book cover design: Francine Eden Platt • Eden Graphics, Inc.

Book cover photo: Timothy Eberly • unsplash.com

Published by
Never Alone Publishing
Fort Wayne, IN

Never Alone
PUBLISHING

For I know the plans I have for you," declares the LORD, *"plans to prosper you and not to harm you, plans to give you hope and a future.*

Jeremiah 29:11 NIV

Dedications

This book is dedicated to:

Katte and David
Kitte and Mike
Jessica
Maisy Rose
George, Lois, Carol, Philip
Georgiann

In loving memory:

Mom and Dad
Aunt Bessie
My sweet sister, Clara

Forward

What a humble honor to pen this forward for Phyllis Bex, who was once a stranger but now a friend.

As the local newspaper editor, I was forwarded Phyllis' contact information years ago by a family friend who said Phyllis may have interest in contributing to the newspaper as a columnist, so I reached out, gave her the particulars of the weekly assignment, and asked for a few writing samples.

After reading her work, I quickly realized she has what so many self-professed writers do not—"voice." Her writing style was engaging, entertaining and best of all, welcoming. I felt as though I knew her without ever having met her, and I have no doubt she could write about an afternoon spent watching paint dry, and readers would be engrossed from the start.

But the columns that follow offer far more than that. They represent a wonderful spectrum of writings and ramblings that take readers on a journey to countless destinations. They're often humorous, sometimes poignant but always delightful, full of wit, candor, and heart.

As with all of us, life includes the highs and the lows, the blessings, and challenges.

Phyllis doesn't shy away from any of it, offering a take on life as only she can, from the simple and straightforward to the trials and troubles.

My hope is that readers will enjoy the nostalgic retrospectives from life down on the farm as much as I did, that they will appreciate the insights that come from a fascinating life that started in rural America and concluded in corporate America.

So, join me, will you, as we dive into the pages that follow and enjoy a journey back in time, a glimpse into yesteryear—and insights into "Life on Turkeyneck Hill."

— Stephen Crane
Editor of *Morgan Country Correspondent,*
Martinsville, IN

A Note from the Author

The following pages will transport you on a nostalgic journey of stories from long ago. They are a collection of columns I've written for the local newspaper in Martinsville, Indiana. All have been edited or updated to provide clarity. Some of the stories contain related photos to capture a thousand words. It is my pleasure to share these narratives in book form.

In these columns, my attempt is to tell stories of my childhood recollections with additional memories from my siblings while being raised on a working farm. The farm is still owned and operated by our brother Philip and his family.

Hopefully, the stories will bring a little chuckle, cause you to reminisce, stimulate a conversation, or all three. The lighthearted yet sometimes tongue-in-cheek stories occasionally turn serious. Nevertheless, that is the way of life—it turns serious when least expected.

Most of all, I am honored that you chose to select my book and read my stories. Thank you. My desire is that you share them with others and keep hope alive. May you be blessed as you hear my voice talk about "Life on Turkeyneck Hill." Enjoy!

Phyllis Dow Bex, Author

CONTENTS

In the Beginning

Happenstances of Country Life

Developing Understandings

County and State Fairs

Remembering Our Loved Ones

Thanksgiving Memories

Christmas Memories

Other Holiday Fun

In The Beginning

When Harry met Dortha

Do you sometimes wonder how couples meet and begin their courtship? This is the story of our parents when they were young and how they met in 1938.

Our mother, Dortha, grew up in the small community of Gosport along with her three sisters and parents. The rolling landscape of this quiet and quaint town is full of friendly people. The water tower directly across the street from their home is a landmark with the name *GOSPORT* written in big bold letters. Back then, the tent factory and sawmills were thriving industries, providing many jobs. In the heart of downtown stood a corner drugstore with the old-time soda fountain and a short order menu. Sometimes we went there for ice cream. That's a fond memory.

In the center of town there is a little park with a huge gazebo where we played as kids. Of course, there was the 5 and 10 cent store along with a hardware. The feed mill and grain bins along the river were busy hubs in this farming community. Cargo boats ran up and down the river with the grain and other harvest trading at this port. Hence the name, Gosport. In fact, our ancestor, Ephraim Goss was a great-grandfather of our maternal grandmother, he founded the town.

Gosport water tower

Just north of Dortha's home on the main drag was a gas station which also had groceries well before its time. It was called "Briggs," probably because the owners' last name was "Briggs." I remember that store well, as it had penny candy and delicious grape jelly in a round white cardboard container.

The town was in its prime when Dortha was young until many years into her adulthood. Like many small towns and communities of old, they're now broken, run down, and in need of a good facelift. Most people migrated to the bigger cities where jobs were plentiful, and "the living was easy."

Dortha and her sisters always found joy and laughter when they were together until each one left this life. The youngest sister, Mary, was the last to remain until the age of 93. Their sense of humor was authentic and came naturally.

Teenager Aunt Mary at the base of the tower

They enjoyed singing and harmonized well as a group. Mary was a good yodeler, as it was a popular art form in her younger years. After their children were all adults and gone, Dortha and Mary were on a country music radio station bus trip from Indianapolis to Nashville, TN. On the way, they commandeered the bus microphone and sang a few songs. They were excellent

2

vocalists for amateurs. Other travelers on the bus yelled for more. Someone asked, "Do you perform and what is your stage name?" After some thought, Dortha said, "We are the Apple Sisters, I'm Corey and this is Seedy." Of course, she made that up.

L to R Aunt Lucy, Aunt Martha, Mom, Aunt Mary

Our dad, Harry, was a country boy from a farm of four hundred plus acres in the neighboring county. He grew up loving to farm and learned everything from his father while they worked the land together. Harry lived on the farm along with his parents and younger sister, Bessie. Harry called the farm home his whole life. It is still in the family under our brother Philip's management.

Kris Angela (Lois's daughter), Mom, and Aunt Mary when they returned from the bus trip

At one time, the farm had three separate homes. The "big house," as it was called, was the main home. It was the one which burned to the ground in 1956. Up the road a hundred yards, was a small home where Harry lived after he was married. It was warmly called the "little house. "At the top of Turkeyneck Hill stood a little three-room house with three porches where his Grandpa Goss lived, his mother's family. That was where Harry's

3

mother was raised. Her father was the Reverend George Goss, a Baptist minister who loved *flower gardens*. That house was called the Grandpa Goss house.

Dad tending sheep as a teenager

Harry's dad, Uncle Charlie as he was affectionately called, was a gentle-spirited man who worked diligently to make the barnyard look like a Norman Rockwell painting. Everything was always put away, the grass mowed, and weeds gone. My dad's painting, if there was one, didn't quite reflect the same charm.

Dad's parents
Charlie and Alice Dow

Great Grandma and Grandpa Goss
with Dad and Aunt Bessie

Harry's parents were older when they began a family, and as a result, he and his sister were spoiled. Some call it love. Though Harry was a bit of a wild child, he respected his parents and worked hard at all he did. His little sister, Bessie, left home to work at Farm Bureau Co-Op in Indianapolis after her high school graduation.

Now for the juicy part. One refreshing springtime, when young hearts were looking for love, Dortha and her friend Mary were going on a double date. Dortha's date was with Malcolm, and his cousin, Harry, went with Mary. Harry and Dortha hardly knew each other, and neither did Mary and Malcolm.

Harry drove his car, a Model T Ford. The two couples had a lovely evening on their dates. However, as the night concluded, Harry delivered each one to their home. Since Dortha was the last

Grandpa and Grandma with Dad and Aunt Bessie

one remaining in the car, Harry invited her to sit up front with him. The sparks flew between them, and the rest is history.

As it turned out, Mary and Malcolm were sweet on each other as well. It must have been love at first sight, for in no time, Malcolm and Mary were married. Shortly after their wedding, Harry and Dortha married in September of the same year. This precious story was told to me by my dad when I was a little girl.

Dad's 1936 graduation photo

Mom 1937 before she married Dad

Unfortunately, neither marriage lasted long, and both took new spouses to live out the rest of their lives. Wait, did you want to know this part of the story? Well, Mom and Dad were married for twenty years. Dad married again for two years, was separated, but never divorced, then passed in 1982. Mom married again for 32 years until she died, in 1991.

The best part is Mom and Dad had the *Big Six*. That is what my siblings and I call each other because there are six of us. Yes indeed, we are the best part of this story! Right?

Top L-R, George, Clara, Lois
Bottom-Philip, Phyllis, Carol

Aunt Bessie and Rainwater

This year, Spring has finally sprung and with it came plenty of rain. I know for the farmer and other sunny day workers; the timing of rain means everything. Too much rain can wreak havoc. Of course, later in the summer, low amounts of rainfall can be devastating.

Many people once incorporated rainwater for multiple uses around their homes and farms. Nowadays, people have forgotten the fine elements which exist in rainwater. God provides a good pH balance and alkaline for plants, trees, and grass to grow competently rather than using other types of watering, such as well water or city water.

Though we have had a good dose of rain and storms this year, our eyes dance at all the blooming flowers with their brilliant colors. Even NASA SpaceX will delay their launches because of rainy conditions.

Speaking of which, we have come a long way and have so much further to go in our space exploration. It is fortunate to have the private sector currently funding it.

Back on the farm, well before I could remember, rainwater was collected. It was caught in cisterns and some captured rainwater in barrels. A cistern is an artificial reservoir like an underground tank for storing liquids and especially rainwater. However, some desert states limit the amount of rain that can be collected. Now that is a mystery to me, but I don't know the laws for rainwater runoff.

Clara said, "Back in the 1930s and '40s, Aunt Bessie used rainwater to shampoo her hair when she still lived at home. She had long hair and used Breck shampoo." George remembered, "Aunt Bessie went in the back yard just beyond the kitchen door. There stood a concrete square three feet high. The bottom was filled with rocks where the downspout from the gutter emptied. This rainwater filtered to the cistern below. Near the concrete square stood a hand pump. Aunt Bessie pumped the cistern water into a bucket for shampooing her hair in the yard."

An old cistern pump

This was years before my time, but I can only imagine the site. Aunt Bessie was always so proper and meticulous about everything. I can visualize her in action. She unbraided her long hair and used a dipping cup to pour the tepid water over her head and long hair. Next she gently applied her shampoo. Aunt Bessie gracefully cleaned the length as she massaged the shampoo all over her hair and scalp. Of course, she used the dipping cup once more to rinse her flowing hair until the hair was squeaky clean. Back then, a head of wet hair only air dried.

Aunt Bessie's graduation photo 1939 with her crown of braids.

Our Grandpa Charles Dow did not want his daughter to cut her hair and she honored his request. "Her long braids wrapped around the crown of her head are shown in her senior picture," replied Lois. After Aunt Bessie graduated from high school in 1939, she worked at Farm Bureau Co-op in Indianapolis and wore her hair like that until Grandpa's death in 1951.

In 1948, Grandpa fell and broke his hip. Clara, age nine, recalls, "I remember I was returning to the house from the barnyard. Grandpa was laying along the lane beside our garden. He was scratched up and bleeding. Immediately, I searched and found Dad." Eight-year-old George said, "I was with him when he fell. He climbed over the fence carrying a five-gallon bucket. In my eight-year-old mind, I felt bad because I thought I could have prevented Grandpa from falling."

Aunt Bessie left her job in Indy to care for her dad at home as her mother, our Grandma Alice Dow had already passed in 1942. They delivered a hospital bed for him to the house. He recovered in the comfort of his living room near the kitchen. My only memory of Grandpa Dow was him in a wooden rocking chair rocking me sitting on his lap. Alongside the rocker was a five-gallon metal bucket that Grandpa spat into from his chewing tobacco.

I don't remember the bed, but I can only imagine all the kids were in awe of a hospital bed in the house. Kids weren't allowed in hospitals in those days. We only knew of feather beds which fluff up large then go down to nothing when you get in bed.

After Grandpa died, Aunt Bessie resumed her work in Indianapolis—but first she cut her hair. While still braided, she cut it above the braid and stored it in a bag. She kept it all those years.

When Aunt Bessie passed, Lois asked Clara and me, "Don't you remember she shaped the braids like a crown when it was cut? We placed the braided crown on the pillow with her in the casket."

Debbie said, "I didn't know Bessie kept her hair and that it was buried with her. It's funny the things people put into coffins with their loved ones."

I told all my siblings, "I don't remember her hair." Carol reminded me, "Remember when we cleaned out her apartment, and we found the braids in a plastic bag? Perhaps because we just celebrated her eighty-ninth birthday the day before she died. We were all still in shock, especially at the funeral. We lost her so unexpectedly, as we thought Aunt Bessie would live forever."

"Oh yeah, Carol, you have a point, now I remember the plastic bag," I replied.

My fun-loving brother, George, looking for comic relief retorted, "I remember a comedian back in the day who responded to someone saying, 'You have a point, but if you keep your hat on, no one will notice.' I think it was Woody Woodbury. Phyllis, your comment reminded me of that line."

Much of this information was from the Big Six's current group texts. We share information and genuinely enjoy reminiscing about our past together.

Although rain is usually perceived as negative, we are grateful for the rain. Like the air we breathe, water is second as most needed. One thing is for sure, Aunt Bessie sure made a difference in our lives as we enjoyed her stories, especially after our dad died in 1982.

But for now, shouldn't we all collect rainwater and shampoo our hair in the yard? If only I could find a barrel, bucket, and hand pump, eh?

Farm Life Isn't for Sissies

Our parents, Harry, twenty, and Dortha, seventeen, were married in 1938. They moved to the *little house* on the farm up the road from the main house. The main house was always called the *big house* where Dad's parents lived; it was the house nearest the barnyard. This farm was special. Our ancestors' desire was for it

The big house from the road.

to remain in the family for generations to come. Currently, that desire has become a reality through Philip and his family.

It wasn't long before Mom was with child and gave birth to Clara, the first grandchild for doting parents and grandparents.

One year old photo of Clara, always a happy disposition.

Soon after Clara's birth, Mom was expecting again. Fourteen months later, George was born. And that's the way it went until they had six children in less than ten years. As a result, there definitely is another generation to inherit the farm. Inheritance was a long time away at that time.

All of us were born as healthy single births. Praise God! Taking care of children kept Dortha busy for a long time. She learned quickly how to stretch every penny so the family would have plenty to go around. Mom was good at her job of parenting, and she loved it. We always felt loved when she was around.

Harry labored hard on the farm with the crops and the livestock. The farm had the Duroc bred of hogs and Polled Hereford cattle.

Duroc hog, Polled Hereford cattle, the Old Cow barn with the silo, the corn crib beyond the hog.

Of course, the agriculture grains were corn, soybeans, wheat, oats, and hay. The chicken house was full of chickens laying eggs. We also raised chickens to fry. We had fresh young tender chicken fried up in a cast iron skillet, um-hmm! It doesn't get much better than that! Let's not forget the milk cow. She was not a Polled Hereford but a Jersey cow. We had plenty of milk to drink, cream for coffee and cereal, and churned butter. Most farms were self-sustaining like ours back in those days.

Across the lane next to the house stood a huge garden where we harvested and preserved many vegetables. We put the potatoes in the cellar, so they'd keep until we needed them. The lettuce, radishes, cucumbers, and other vegetables couldn't be preserved. However, sometimes we made pickles out of the cucumbers. We had an orchard with apple and peach trees behind the barn next to the pasture. Our ancestors made sure the farm was self-sustaining. Food was always plentiful. We had a healthy start. Sounds like a picture-perfect Norman Rockwell painting doesn't it? Well, not so fast.

Even with all the goodness and bounty we had, times could be hard on the family. Some years there were droughts, floods, or storms. Frustrations resulting from too much work and not enough help. The livestock would get sick, and several would die. Sometimes they died while giving birth. Occasionally, the sows and cows decide to go in the woods to give birth in the dead of winter. Newborns could freeze to death out in the bitter freezing weather. That is the life of farming. Farming is a balancing act. Often big risks yield big losses. When the risks paid off, the yield was exceptionally good. A smart farmer learns to budget everything all the time.

Our dad was amazing with all his knowledge of farming for that period. He graduated in 1936 from Paragon High School.

The Paragon School. Dad, Aunt Bessie and all six siblings attended.

Dad read the stars and sky to know the weather coming the next day. He scrutinized the *Farmer's Almanac* and most often it was correct. Dortha, like most mothers, tried to create a very comforting environment for the family as much as possible. Often she helped outside on the farm as well. It was a hard life; it's never intended for weak at heart. That is why only brother, Philip, still farms. He loves farming and everything that goes with it. Bless his heart, the rest of us must be sissies. I for one, prefer the easier life in the suburbs.

One frigid winter, Dad hunted for a sow (a mother pig) that chose to leave the warmth of the barn to have her pigs in the woods. By the time he found her, the momma sow was dead, and the little pigs were close to being frozen to death. He put them in a gunny sack and carried them to the house. Dad gave those lifeless pigs to Mom. He said to Mom, "If you warm them up, they might live. After you feed and raise them, when they are sold, you can have the money to spend however you wish." Mom got all the kids involved and all the pigs survived. We raised them in our kitchen pantry until spring arrived. Then they went outside until they got big enough for the market. Mom bought us our very first black and white TV with the money from those little "almost-dead" pigs.

George sitting on a big Duroc hog as a child.

Those were good memories. The work ethic and survival skills learned from working on the farm is still with us.

15

A Team of Wild Horses

Back in the good old days, (in the spring of 1946) when my brother George was six and Clara seven, they accompanied our dad on the farm in a box wagon. A box wagon is one that is narrow yet has high side boards. It is used for hauling grain. While driving a team of horses from a box wagon, the driver stands up in the wagon. If the wagon is full of grain, the driver sits on the grain.

On this day, the wagon was being pulled by a team of work horses named Prince and Bess. Dad did some fence work in a locust grove near the block building.

An example of a box wagon

When the work was complete, Dad jumped out of the wagon to open the gate. George was to drive the horses through. Then Dad would shut the gate and get back into the wagon. That was the plan.

Something spooked those gentle giants, and they bolted off. They dashed around the big cow barn toward another gate that was shut and proceeded to bust right through it. The horses were picking up speed while they kept scurrying through the barnyard. Both kids were filled with fright, as little George hung onto the reins for dear life, pulling back, trying to make them stop. Clara, on the other hand, screamed her head off in fear. That screaming kept the horses agitated.

Now, the horses ran past the front of the old barn near the windmill where our water pump was housed. At the entrance to the barnyard was another gate. That gate was shut as well, and

the horses ran through it like it was made of balsa. From that point, it was a straight 100-yard downhill grade which teed at the gravel county road.

A team of work horses, not ours

As they ran past the big house where we lived, our Grandpa Charlie Dow was at the window watching them run down the driveway approaching the road. For whatever reason, the horses turned left. When they made their turn, the box wagon was skidding, and up on two wheels. The wagon landed on all four wheels and up the road they went.

Meanwhile, Dad took a shortcut by running across the field from the block building to the house, hoping to cut them off, but to no avail. He knew if they went another mile from home,

Turkeyneck Hill, the drop off on the left

they would be at the top of Turkeyneck Hill. Turkeyneck is steep, curvy, and narrow in places. Dad felt they would surely crash over the edge. On the side of the road is a cliff that is 170 to 200 feet to the bottom — with no guardrail.

Dad drove the car to chase down the wild horses with his prize possessions on board. About a quarter mile from home there was a sharp right turn which sloped downward like a turn on a NASCAR track. The right horse, Bess, got stuck in the muddy ditch on the inside of the turn and went down. That was a good thing because the wagon stopped. But as Dad got to the corner, he stopped the car also on that incline. When he got out, his car door slammed loudly, which spooked the horses again. Up out of the ditch Bess arose and away they ran on down the road. Furthermore, when Bess went down, it pulled her reins out of George's little hand. So, he only had one set of reins.

They continued through the holler, across the culvert, and up the rise to another straight part of the road just before Turkeyneck

At the culvert, the opening at the top is where the horses stopped.

Hill. Little George kept pleading with his sissy, "Be quiet, you are only scaring the horses!" But that didn't stop her, as Clara was petrified. Prince was on the left and so George was pulling with all his might to guide him to the ditch. At the top of the little rise, he got Prince over. There was a medium-sized tree growing about three feet out from the fence but not quite in the road. Prince ran on the fence side of the tree and Bess on the other. The tongue of the wagon nailed the tree and they stopped at last. What a wild ride!

Dad took the children back to the house and the horses to the barnyard. The tongue had broken on the wagon, so Dad replaced it. Then he took the team for a full speed run on the gravel county road in the other direction. They ran for a mile straight, turned around and ran back home at full speed. Prince and Bess's tongues were hanging out as they turned into our lane. Our dad was angry and scared at the same time. If those horses wanted to run, he thought, he'd get it out of their system, so he did.

As of this writing, George is eighty-three and Clara went to heaven in 2021 at age eighty-one. We miss her deeply. Yes, that was back in the good old days on the farm. For all the things we experienced on the farm, it is a wonder we all made it to adulthood.

Birth Order and Subsequent Personalities

Our family of origin often dictates our personalities and can affect our success or failure in life. The order of our birth within the family is something that can never be fully predicted. Just the same, here we are.

I'm quite sure our parents got married in a fever. Their courtship was a wild and predictable romance. Ah yes, good ole Harry and Dortha. Once they were married, they began producing children like there was a race or contest.

Psalm 127:4 tells us, "Like arrows, in the hands of a warrior, are children born in one's youth." Dad quoted that to me when I asked him why we had six kids so fast. I wasn't sure I understood his meaning, but I knew he needed lots of help on the farm and we were free labor.

Clara is the firstborn child and first grandchild of our family. Her birth was just before our beloved Aunt Bessie Dow graduated from Paragon High School in 1939. She beamed with pride that Clara attended her graduation ceremony. Because of that, jokingly, Aunt Bessie said Clara was her favorite.

Fourteen months later, George made his arrival. At last, a son which Mom and Dad were both hoping for. A son to continue the family name and one to be the heir to the family farm. He was the one in whom Mom beamed with pride her entire life. Her golden child—bless his heart. What a spunky little guy he was then and still is a fun personality to this day.

After two years and five days, Lois made a grand entrance by being the largest baby born of the siblings. She weighed over ten pounds. However, she proved to be the smallest in stature of all six as an adult. Lois showed that birthweight is not always an indicator of development.

Lois has always been the one who enjoyed accessorizing her outfits, our little glamour queen while young. Being a precocious youngster, she has yet to meet a stranger to this day.

Now, Carol made a quiet arrival over two years from Lois. Her arrival was just in time for the fall harvest. Her personality is quiet and observant. Moreover, she was the smartest one in schoolwork of all the siblings. I guess she just paid greater attention than the rest of us while in class; or I didn't know my other siblings' scholastic merits. I do know Carol's homemaking skills were very tactical, and she has used them her entire life.

Sweet Philip came just in time for Thanksgiving two years later. He grew to be tall, strong, and always followed big brother George on the farm. His love for farming was greater compared to the rest of us. He and his family remain on the farm to this day. Philip's faithfulness to keep the farm intact is impressive. As it were, the second son was the heir to the farm because everyone else *got out of dodge* after high school.

The best birth was the last. Mine. They liked to call me the *baby*, but I was merely the youngest of the litter. As is the case, I was treated as a token. Often that was a good thing, but most times not. It was tough to get attention unless I clowned around a lot and that became a habit. Nevertheless, I felt like the tail end of a crack the whip game as time rolled by.

Consequently, all the studies show the firstborn is the leader. Well, Clara led by having her family. Then all our family get-togethers were held at her home for years after our parents died. Clara was always sure to look after me when needed. That was so special to be in her care.

George, being the first son, really became the "boss" in the siblings. Yet he was away after high school to serve in the navy for twenty years. He found remarkable success serving in the navy along with his engineering career following his navy retirement. So, his behavior lines up with the studies.

Lois was one of the middle children, but her outgoing personality afforded her attention unlike the predictable middle children. She was closer to Dad; she also didn't fear him like the rest. Lois excelled with her career in business. Her many interests gave her a strong influence in the family and community as well.

Carol was a typical middle child. She didn't desire much attention. However, she excelled in school and other projects she pursued especially with the sewing machine and crafts. As an adult, she drove a school bus for over thirty years and was home when her children were home. Then she continued to serve the

school by driving her route, plus drove many field and sport trips. Carol and her husband, Jim, once had a huge

Aunt Bessie and Carol, as a teen, in the dining room of the new house

garden where they preserved many fruits and vegetables.

The tenderness Philip continually showed me was impeccable. He was my guard and protector. Philip relished serving in that role. His love for track and field showed as he excelled in pole vaulting in high school. He was a whiz at driving cars, dragging on Strawberry Lane. Philip was my hero as a kid. The birth order for him only caused him to strive for excellence. He found it in farm life with his wife. He served in the Navy like George, but only for four years. Philip still loves the farm and serves the community in many ways.

As the last in the family is me. I fit the profiles perfectly. I am the clown, the salesperson, the adventurer, and the seeker of thrills. Therefore, I suppose what they say about the youngest is correct. Unfortunately, the last one standing can be a disappointing place. It was always a sad day to watch as everyone left home. I hope to live a long life, but I want my remaining siblings to live long with me.

23

I will say that all six of us have been great successes in life.

We all love the Lord, serve our communities, and are happy. The next generation is a total of twenty cousins, the next generation after those cousins and the next

Stair-steps: L to R, Clara, George, Lois, Carol, Philip, and Phyllis

generation are still growing. But they all would make our parents proud. It is amazing what the power of prayer does for our children, and children to come. So, parents, keep praying for all children. God honors a fervent and prayerful heart.

The scripture in Joel 1:3 tells us, "Tell it to your children, and let your children tell it to their children, and their children to the next generation." That is what has gone on for generations from our grandparents and beyond, on down to our great-grandchildren. We are still praying blessings for our generations to come.

Cows, Disking, Corn, and Silos

Our dad was a genius. He always had plenty of work for us to do. His two-fold intent was to keep us busy and out of trouble. Second, chores were accomplished which were essential for farming.

Besides feeding the animals in the barn yards and fields, we *got* to help with many other chores. I remember many times, our pastured cows got out. Neighbors often called to tell us, "Your cows are out." We'd get them in and must repair the fence where they broke through. Hence, we learned fence building. At times, the cows got out after a storm had knocked a tree over the fence. Therefore, we learned how to saw a tree or use an axe. Unfortunately, the cows getting out happened a lot. As adult siblings, on April Fool's Day we still call each other to say, "The cows are out," even though we no longer live on the farm.

When spring had sprung, we'd prepare and till the fields for planting. I never plowed, but Philip plowed and disked. Later after Philip left for the Navy, I did 100 percent of the disking.

A current day disk and tractor, fancier than the one I drove

For your information, the disk implement is rows of concave-shaped round metal plates about 20-25 inches in diameter. The sharp edge is like a knife for slicing through the soil. The width is usually about 10-12 feet wide with two rows of disks on their edge. One row is cutting to the right and the other to the left. The disk is pulled behind a tractor to break apart and level the soil after plowing.

We had a two-row corn picker attached to the tractor. It had an elevator angled over the wagon which was hitched to the tractor. The ear corn would drop into the wagon as it was picked.

In today's modern technology, a combine harvests corn several rows at a time. The corn stalk is cut by the machine, going into the combine. This machine is so smart, it separates the corn from the stalk and puts the stalk through a chopper then spits it out behind. It takes the ear of corn, shells it with the corn kernels going into the reservoir. The cobs get spit out the back as well. Pretty neat, huh?

Picking 8 rows at a time, or 35 feet wide when combining soybeans. It is equipped with computers and all sorts of modern devices. Philip's granddaughter, Annalei harvested with this one. (Photos courtesy of Terri Dow)

When I was a youngster, Dad had me walk behind the wagon while he drove the two-row corn-picker. My job was to pick up ears of corn that were left on the ground. I hated that job.

I really did. What kept my interest is the act of throwing the ear of corn to the wagon. I would imagine I was on the playground throwing a ball at someone. The fantasy played out in my mind every time I followed the wagon. Without a doubt, this was Dad's way of keeping me fit and out of trouble. That picker missed a lot of corn, and I did, too.

Have you ever wondered what goes into those 100-foot-tall skinny round silos that are next to barns? Many different things, but what we put in them was called ensilage.

Dad planted a mix of sorghum with the corn. The corn is cut off at the ground with a forage harvester. This machine chops it up then blows it in the huge wagon or forage wagon trailing the chopper. Our ensilage had the sweetness of sorghum and the heartiness of corn which smelled terrible as it fermented for winter feed, but the cattle loved it.

The silo next to the Big White Barn. George tending the hogs.

Next to the silo was a contraption called a silo blower. The massive fan of the blower propels the mixture through the tall piping leading to the roof of the silo. The ensilage settles down and eventually the bulkiness of the fibrous fodder fully fills the silo. How'd you like that fun thrill of *F* words?

Note: While the silo is being filled, someone is inside stomping and packing the silage down so there will be no air gaps.

That is an extremely dangerous job. As the ensilage rises, they shut one of the silo doors. Repeating this all the way to the top.

Once the silo is filled, we wait for the fermentation to occur. By the time the snow flies and all the natural grass forage is depleted, ensilage will be fermented and ready to feed the cattle.

The doors of the silo are made of 36" concrete squares with full bodied crisscross hinges which we used to climb. The area is enclosed to create a chute for the ensilage to fall. Climbing up the tall chute of the silo, we arrive at the top and open the first door. The door opens with the twisting of a lock, pushing it inside, and at last, the work begins. Using a wide pitchfork, layer by layer, we threw ensilage down the chute. The aroma of the corn and sorghum after fermentation is very pungent. Like sauerkraut only nastier.

At the floor level, we filled large, galvanized tubs full of ensilage and carried them to the long feeder troughs while the cattle were lowing outside. Once we have filled the troughs with ensilage, we swiftly open the sliding door. The cattle fight their way to the troughs, devouring the steaming candy-like ensilage on the frosty winter days.

Yes, Dad was a wise man. Though his methods seemed hard, we learned volumes being involved on the farm and we are all grateful for the life lessons. Not only that, but we also kept our bodies fit.

What's in a Name?

When you are born number six in the family, I'm guessing parents might run out of relatives to use as namesakes.

The first two siblings in our family were named after our grandparents. Our grandmothers were Clara Gayle Stierwalt and Minerva Alice Dow. As a result, the firstborn daughter was named Clara Alice. Just think, she could have been labeled Minerva Gayle.

Our grandpa was Charles Clay Dow and great-grandpa was George Goss. Hence, George Clay is the firstborn son's name.

None of the rest of us were named after anyone except for Carol who was named after our mother, Dortha. Sister Dorothy Carol goes by her middle name Carol.

Mom loved the name Lois. Since she was born in the month of May, Mom named her "Lois May." After Philip Leon, I came along.

Mom had the name Sondra picked out for me. She wanted to call me *Sonny* until her dad suggested, "If you have a little girl, I think she should be named Phyllis to go with Philip." Bless his heart, Grandpa died of a heart attack the day I was born, so the name Phyllis was used. Poor Sonny didn't stand a chance.

I've heard of people giving their babies three or four names and then their surname. If you are born Catholic, you receive another name at confirmation. We were not Catholic, so we are stuck with our names.

I asked family members and friends of their name sakes and got various responses.

For example, brother-in-law Dick said, "I was named after the family mule. They had mules named Bob and Dick. My brother's name is Bob." I'm not sure if this is the truth, but I do know Dick's mother's name was Clyde. She was surely named by a family ancestor or after another mule.

Many people use biblical names when naming their offspring. What an impressive way to pay tribute to their faith. Sometimes, the name is a lot to live up to, especially if their name is *Jesus*. I only hope they honor the holy names.

Often the firstborn son is named after the father as a Jr. If the Jr. then has a son and gives his son his name, they become the 3rd or III. Consequently, I have heard them being nicknamed *Trip* as a result. Wonder if they become a Jr. when Grandpa dies? Nah, I think not.

What did we know when we named our children? Being only twenty-one when I had my twins, I was set on naming them something unique. Katte Louise, (Louise after an aunt) and Kitte Leone (after Uncle Philip Leon). What I didn't predict was how they would forever be spelling their name or correcting errant spellings.

When I had my third child, I made it easy. Jessica Ann's namesake is after my middle name, Ann. Jessi recently informed me, "When I get married, I plan to drop the 'Ann' and keep my surname name along with my husband's last name."

When she told us her plan, I had a look of horror and disbelief on my face. She announced this in person to a group of us, not thinking about me and how displaced I might have felt. Upon her realization, she burst out in hearty laughter. Frankly, I didn't see the humor, but it's okay, I know what her birth certificate reads.

"What's in a name? That which we call a rose. By any other name would smell as sweet." Shakespeare's *Romeo and Juliet*. The phrase implies a name means little, whereas the person's character is more important.

The Big Six front to back. Mom was quite the photographer.

Always try to be mindful of who, what, and where you come from. Make the most of what you have. It's more important to do your best with the name you've been given, whether you have a good name or not.

Turkeyneck Hill, Cow Tipping, and Snipes

Since I have been writing about "Life on Turkeyneck Hill" for some time now, I should reveal if the hill truly exists. You might have tried to find it on a map. Could it be among the myths like "cow tipping or snipe hunting?" Maybe.

If you have tried to find "Turkeyneck Hill" on a map, I hope it was an old one. On most newer maps, it is not there. Some wise guy decided to change the road names a few years back. Why did he do that? We liked the old names, didn't we? Some of the names were made up by the locals, and the names stuck through the generations. Country folk like that sort of thing.

However, when calling an ambulance during emergencies, they needed better ways to find people. The driver needs to know exactly where they were going. Time is *of the essence* and important to save lives during a 911 response call. They need all the 411 so they can ETA for a HA (heart attack). That is why the road names were changed.

Most county roads are numbers. They are broken down into 25-unit increments. A "25-unit" equals a fourth of a mile. North, south, east, and west correspond with the division roads. Also, the address ending with even numbers are on the north or west sides of the roads. In case you don't remember fourth grade math, an even number is divisible by two. The odd number addresses are on the south and east side of the roads. This is my educational portion for today.

But what the heck? Map or no map, the *old timers* still call Base Line Road *Turkeyneck Hill Road*. It's on top of the big hill right after you turn west off Strawberry Lane! As a matter of fact, *Base Line Road* is the same lateral as Morgan Street in Martinsville. I know you like a little Morgan County trivia.

Wait, what?—Strawberry Lane? Well, that road, *our old drag strip*, has a new name as well. This renaming could go on forever! Thus, I will stop for now.

Turkeyneck Hill going up. No, there are no turkeys around it.

The truth is, Turkeyneck Hill is about three miles northwest of Paragon going west toward Samaria Baptist Church and Porter's Cave.

What about that cow tipping? Again, a myth. The game was for the non-farming sort who would go to the farm at night in search for a herd or a few cows asleep standing up. Supposedly, they would sneak up on the cow and push them over. Hence the name, cow tipping.

For those of you who don't know, cows don't sleep standing up. They might take a nap, a cow powernap. But for that deep REM sleep, they lie down. Really, sorry to burst your bubble.

Now for snipes. If you have ever been snipe hunting, you have been in for a treat, haven't you? Oh my gosh, I had the best time with this game!

"All city folk should come on out to the country and let's play a game." Tell them to bring a big bag or sack. Preferably, find one of those large brown paper grocery bags. (My older sibling, Lois, used gunny sacks.) Nowadays, you may only find a large paper take-out bag with little paper handles on them because of the plastic invasion. We no longer hear, "paper or plastic" at the checkouts who still bag the groceries.

Next, fold down the top of the sack one roll so it will stay open. This game can only be played in the dark and the darker the better. There are two teams. The team of those who have been snipe hunting and those who have not. Those who haven't been hunting do not know who has or hasn't.

Someone demonstrates how to hunt by lowering the bag to the ground and yells "Here snipe, here snipe." Tell the hunter that the harmless *snipe* will come to you and jump in the bag. I liked it best when I told the big burly guys to say "Here snipey, snipey, snipey," "Here snipey, snipey, snipey." They all practiced the *call* before going into the dark woods. Plus, no flashlights were allowed because the snipes are afraid of bright light.

But of course, there are no snipes. No such thing. There are many variations of the game and they all work. The ones who hunted them had fun, and the ones who watched had *more* fun. I know, it wasn't nice, but we weren't being bullied, we were just having fun. Some may think that was unfair to the rookie, but we didn't.

Now you know more about Turkeyneck Hill than you wanted to know, plus two crazy games.

Creeks, Sledding, and a Boat ride

The creek on our farm was far from being deep enough to swim, but we still went swimming. It was a long walk to the creek, so at times, we'd drive the tractor down the hill. We called that road, the *tractor/wagon* road. It was carved among the trees from the top edge of the woods down to the creek bottoms. During the rare *off* times from farming duties, in the heat of summer, we'd go to the creek. Good times were had unless we disturbed a nest of snakes or snapping turtles, then it wasn't much fun.

Driving up and down the steep hill was scary, although we did it several times. That saved the long-distance drive on the country roads to tend to the fields in the creek bottoms. Naturally, we could have walked from the house all the way down to the creek, but that was no fun.

One summer, we had a huge picnic by the creek after our last day of school. Of course, our picnic would be on a blanket or simply sitting on the ground as there were no tables. We took the tractor and wagon as well as our big stock truck full of families for a picnic. Besides our family of eight, Joyce and Ralph Wilson brought their three, Mickey, Karen, and Kathy. Included was Gib and Shirley Bastin, with daughter Ginger. Other families and our Aunt Bessie joined the fun. Taking a picnic basket full of food to share along the creek bank was a treat. In those days, most of our meals were served at the kitchen table.

Speaking of the tractor/wagon road; it made a suitable place to go snow sledding. However, we didn't have a sled. Our neighbor friends brought their sleds of many kinds. Philip took a piece of tin which had blown off the barn roof. He bent it back about ten inches on the front edge. As we sat down and grabbed onto the sharp sides with our holey gloves, down the slippery slope we'd go. We learned to guide the tin sled by leaning one way or the other. Often, our sled was much faster than anything else and quite a thrill as a result. If the going was too dangerous, we just rolled off the tin and let it go. Too dangerous meant we were heading for a tree or a big ravine.

Unfortunately, the tin could cut our frozen exposed hands because of the holey gloves. A little slice didn't stop us, though, we were having a blast in the snow. We doctored many a cut from frozen hands sledding in the cold and snow.

Our parents divorced when I was nine. The kids who were still at home remained to help with the farm. Later, Mom married Bob who wasn't anything like our dad. He worked at a foundry and wasn't a farmer. However, Bob and Mom had a long life together. I guess that was what matters most.

When I was thirteen, I visited Mom while she and Bob lived in Trevlac near Lake Lemon in Brown County. Their home was back a lane on Bean Blossom Creek which led to the lake. I learned to swim in that creek. It had snakes too, but we didn't see them often.

I was up early one Sunday morning. Bob asked me, "Do you want to go for a boat ride?" "Yes!" Of course, I did. We shoved off from the dock as he fired up the small 40 HP outboard engine. It was a sixteen-foot boat that one couldn't ski behind, yet it was swift. The boat had a windshield and steering wheel with four seats. Bob was zipping up the creek for about a block, turned around, then gunned it the other way. Riding in the boat was refreshing on that muggy Sunday morning. I loved it!

After four laps, a lady came to the creek side. She lived five or six houses from Mom and Bob's home. This lady had a freshly lit cigarette stuck between her lips. It bobbled up and down as she yelled profanities and shook her pointed finger at us. Being the gentleman he was, Bob pulled over to her side of the creek bank then shut down the engine. He said, "Yes, ma'am?" All I remember she said, "You little p_ _ _-pots! Don't you know what time it is?" Bob apologized and then slowly boated back home. Once docked, Bob chuckled and whispered to me, "I don't think she likes us!" I ran inside to tell Mom about what happened, and we laughed the entire day.

Though farm labor was hard, we *did* have fun on occasions especially when we went to Mom's house.

Night Sounds in the Country

The sweltering days of summer have always been difficult in Indiana. As children of the 1950s, our country home had all the windows open allowing the cool breeze to flow freely. We had window fans and other oscillating fans blowing especially while we slept. On the other hand, we didn't know any better, so we accepted it. It is amazing what we can accept when we don't know any better.

One thing stands out vividly in my mind are the night sounds. The nightly chorus of the crickets, katydids, and locusts, to name a few, was ever present. After the divorce, my mom left, and when my dad was not home, that sound felt very forlorn. Sure, my siblings were still in the house, but it was lonely. It only got worse as each one graduated and left home. I am the youngest. Currently, I still feel the heart-wrenching loneliness I felt as a child when I hear the country night sounds. So, I don't like to open my windows, I just turn on the air conditioning.

Many folks find cricket sounds soothing and even have it on their sound machines for sleeping. Maybe it reminds them of a good night's sleep when they camped as kids. The sounds of thunderstorms, rain forests, and trickling brooks as well as waves of the ocean are leading sounds for relaxation. Not me, I would rather have a ticking clock.

Sometimes, people open their windows at night for fresh air because the air conditioning isn't on, and the room is a little stuffy. When it is spring, the cool fresh air can be filled with pollen. Some predict this is the perfect recipe for hay fever, or a summer cold. Like I said before, I prefer the windows to be shut with the air on.

With the onset of air conditioning, one rarely hears the night sounds. Some may not even know what I am talking about. These days, most people never open their windows. If they do, they are closed by nightfall. The insects are still making their sounds every night whether we hear them or not. That is like, "If a tree falls in the forest and no one is there to hear it, does it still make a sound?" Yes, it does.

Beginning in the 1960s air conditioning was becoming a comfort to be had. Office buildings were starting to be cooled. The well-to-do were the only ones who cooled their homes. In fact, the creator of cooled air was twenty-five-year-old Willis H. Carrier. This was in 1902 when his invention helped cool an office building in Brooklyn, NY.

It wasn't until 1931 when they invented a cooling unit that rested on the window ledge. The first ones were very expensive, costing $10,000-$50,000. That translates to $120K-$600K in today's money. It is said they were only used by people who didn't sweat, the wealthy.

By the 1950s, post WWII with the economic boom and more modern advances, the home air conditioning unit was becoming more affordable. Over one million in-home units were sold for home use in the '60s. The 1960 United States population was 179 million people.

Finally, in the 1970s, they figured out how to create central air in homes with existing heating systems. However, it didn't become standard in homes for a few decades.

At our schools, there were no air-conditioned classrooms or any other areas. After high school in 1967, I attended a beauty college in Indianapolis. They only had air conditioning in the beauty salon for the paying customers who came to get their hair done.

One of my friends, Becky, rode to beauty school from Brown County with a businessman who worked in Indianapolis. He was a prideful man. Although very few people had air-conditioned cars, he liked to pretend his car did. Once they reached the out skirts of Indy, he told Becky, "Roll the windows up, I don't want anyone to think I don't have air conditioning." The mornings weren't too bad, but the drive home was suffocating until they reached the edge of town where they could open the windows. It is funny what some people do for make believe.

These louvers in the hallway ceiling were similar to ours and it did the job.

I built a new home in 1995 without central air. It did have a whole house attic fan. The

41

ceiling louvers were in the hallway near the bedrooms. That attic fan sucked the cool night air in so strongly the curtains in every room pulled toward the fan. Early in the morning, after turning off the fan, we shut all the windows, blinds, and curtains. Our home remained comfortable until about dinner time. It was a very affordable way to keep our home cool in the heat of summer. The noise of the fan drowned out the night sounds and lulled us into slumber.

In Indiana, we have quite a few hot days every summer. We are creative to find ways to enjoy the summer heat including the night sounds. It has been a long time since those olden days, all is well with my soul now outdoors in the summer.

Happenstances

of

Country Life

The Day Our Home Burned

The early homes of our youth hold a special place in our hearts, wouldn't you agree? My three sisters and two brothers felt especially close to our eighteenth-century farmhouse where we lived. In fact, it was

The East view of the home.

first our Grandma Alice and Grandpa Charles Clay Dow's home where they held the second deed for the land.

Unfortunately, on Friday, August 13, 1956, our three-storied white planked and multi-generational farmhouse burned to the ground. It was a charming home with a lot of character. Our incinerated home was a tragedy for all eight of us. Watching the last embers burn and then smolder was hard to believe or even comprehend. Everything we owned went up in smoke. The only

The Farm Letterhead of Dad and Grandpa, seared on the edges as the fire licked at the desk papers. C.C. stands for Charles Clay. While, "Son" is my dad, Harry Dow.

items saved from the fire were a drainer full of dishes, dried clothes piled on the bed including the chenille bedspread, and Dad's desk full of important papers.

People spoke of how *unlucky* we were because of the date, Friday the thirteenth. However, our family believed in Jesus Christ and had no time for superstitions. It wasn't unlucky at all; it was faulty wiring that caught the house ablaze. Nevertheless, we lost everything.

Carol, my eleven-year-old sister, just happened to be the only one in the home. Dad's cousins, Floyd and Melvin Dow, were building an addition to the chicken house when they noticed smoke flowing from the house chimney and went in the home to check. As they entered, smoke already filled the home. Floyd used our wall-mounted crank phone to call the fire department as he hunkered low to breathe.

Carol made sure they saved Dad's desk, including the important paperwork, and they grabbed the other two things. Though she was petrified, Carol had the presence of mind to salvage what was important. She even crawled around on the floor under the heavy smoke calling for our black cocker spaniel pup. The dog scrambled toward her, and she rescued the dog. Because of her quick thinking, we felt Carol was a hero, even at age eleven.

For decades, this beloved home welcomed and entertained countless people from the community. The exterior was like a plantation of the south with tall swaying pine trees caressing the front, a beautiful meadow to the west, and fragrant flowers all around; it had an atmosphere of its own. As guests entered the front door, there stood a beautiful wooden circular staircase with plastered walls curving around it. I remember when my brother Philip and I stood at the top and slung marbles trying to make them hug the wall all the way down. Mom didn't like that, and we were scolded more than once. Guess we were slow learners.

Adjoining the kitchen was a three-sided pantry next to the back door. That out-of-the-way space was where we took our baths in a large, galvanized tub. We had no bathroom except the outdoor privy. At night and in the winter, we

Eating in the kitchen with the back door and pantry beyond. L to R, Philip, Mom, Dad, George, the back of a neighbor boy, Billy.

used a lidded pot. The only running water available was from the kitchen sink. Regardless, we had plenty enough to share.

The home had two large rooms on the first floor with a fireplace positioned in the wall between them with lovely oaken cabinetry and shelving next to the fireplaces in both rooms. Their ceilings featured a large vent allowing heat to radiate to the upstairs. At the bottom of the staircase was a large bedroom claimed by Aunt Bessie. She and my dad were both raised in this home; therefore, it was her home as well, and she slept there when visiting from Indianapolis. The room directly above was hers, too. In both she stored treasures and heirlooms of beautiful glassware, dishes, sewing pieces which our ancestors crafted, old photos, many quilts, hurricane lamps, and wall hangings. We weren't allowed to enter unless invited.

On this sunny summer afternoon, I planned to go swimming with a friend. I was really looking forward to this rare treat. In my childlike mind, my biggest concern when we heard the house was burning was, "Did anyone save my bathing suit I hung on the banister post?" No. My plans were thwarted, but after seeing the total devastation, swimming didn't much matter.

Shortly after breakfast, I'd gone with Mom and my oldest sister Clara, age seventeen, to Martinsville for weekly shopping and running errands. When we stopped in Paragon on the way home, someone informed us, "Your house is on fire!" We lived about four miles from town.

Peering toward the farm, we could barely see any smoke. Mom drove like a woman gone mad. It was a scary ride for me in the back seat. In those days, there were no seat belts. Consequently, I was tossed all over the back seat. A half mile from home when reaching the top of Turkeyneck Hill, we saw massive smoke billowing large black clouds to the heavens. The massive smoke rolled and rose across the fields and forest scarring up the pristine blue skies and puffy white clouds.

Clara screamed and became hysterical. Mom snapped, "Stop it, Clara! Get control of yourself or you will lose the baby!" My seven-year-old mind was spiraling and thought, "What baby?" Unknown to me, Clara was pregnant, and it was too early to share.

Upon arrival, Mom fainted as she pulled into the driveway. Again, my youth didn't know nor understand how Mom felt. Observing her home nearly burnt to the ground was too much for her to cope. What a sight. What a feeling of hopelessness. Everything we had went up in smoke. Now, what would we do?

Another sister, Lois, who was fourteen at the time, spent the night at Kurtz's to babysit their two children. The next morning, she roller skated with the children on their outdoor dance floor while the parents slept. They lived at the top of Denny Hill, across from the Ritter family. Situated due south of our home, Lois and the kids saw the smoke. Lois' worst fears were realized when the Kurtz family took her home. As Lois gazed at our *burnt-to-ground* home, it caused her an emotional emptiness not hard to comprehend.

On this day, Dad left a list of chores for my brothers George (sixteen) and Philip (nine) to complete. Only this time he hired our neighbor Brice to help. When Brice didn't show, George and Philip drove the Farmall H tractor to his house. Brice couldn't start his pickup truck, so George towed him to the top of Turkeyneck Hill. George gave the truck a shove by hand and let gravity take over. As it sped downhill, Brice popped the clutch, starting his truck. Philip and Brice's son Jimmy had already jumped into the bed of the pickup. Brice's older son Billy jumped on the tractor with George heading down the hill to see if his dad's truck was still running at the bottom. There was Brice and the two younger boys—waiting on them with the truck running.

Brice stated, "Boys, I need to get a cold beer at the Blue Ox Tavern in town before I get to work." The boys all tagged along to

Paragon. While waiting on Brice, the two younger boys just *hung out* in town going from place to place. George and Billy walked down the alley to the Standard Oil gas station. It was like a truck stop in the early days. Parked along Highway 67 was a truckload of watermelons. The older boys climbed up the sideboards to steal one. Suddenly, the owner of the truck appeared and threatened, "I'm going to call the sheriff 'if' you don't put that watermelon back on the truck." They complied.

Before long, Brice jumped in the truck and yelled at the boys, "Get in the truck, your house is on fire!" As they raced toward the farm, they saw the smoke. Philip remembers, "Jimmy and I rode in the truck bed. I recall Brice was speeding fast, so we moved to the front of the bed next to the cab and held on tight. When Brice hit the brakes, our fingers were pinched between the cab and the bed. By the time they reached our driveway, all that was left were smoldering embers." George stood amazed and helpless— feeling a bit ashamed of the way he spent his day. Philip stared at the blackness and said nothing.

Unfortunately, Dad had taken a load of livestock to the stockyards in Indianapolis and when he returned home, it was over. All his memories of the many gatherings in this grand home his whole life, plus the relics and antiques from parents and ancestors, were up in smoke. The smoldering embers was all that remained when he arrived. The view was unbelievable. The mountain of a man he was, Dad fell to his knees while holding his face and wept.

The little house on top of Turkeyneck Hill was part of the family farm. This home was where our dad's mother grew up, our Grandma Alice Goss Dow. We affectionately called it the *Grandpa Goss* place. Dad was renting it to the Brice Litton family. They were willing to move, but it took a couple of weeks for them to find new lodging and vacate it for us.

For now, we were homeless. Many families loaned us camp cots, bedding, and simple provisions. There was an old garage with electricity in the barnyard that was empty, so we stayed there. It was built to hold the old horse-drawn carriage of our ancestors. The walls were lined with smooth wood and Dad used it for storing grain when needed. The south side of the garage had two large windows which were open. They didn't even have screens. As we slept, we could feel the dew settling on us in the cool August nights.

One can only imagine what Mom and Dad must have felt, for they never spoke of it in my presence. Although, I don't remember feeling desperate in this hopeless situation, but I'm sure we all felt very empty and needy.

We lived in the Grandpa Goss home for about eighteen months. Eventually, a new one-story ranch home was built on the site where the massive home once stood. Rebuilding anything after a loss takes courage, but we were strong, healthy, and alive.

Our blessing was the community and the church folks who came to our aid and surrounded us with God's love. That is a sign of good neighbors— thankfully, they were plentiful.

God knew what He was doing, even back then. Our sweet niece Debbie was born to Clara seven months later in 1957. She is the first grandchild for Mom and Dad, the first of many offspring to come in our large family. Debbie's life is a blessing and special to all. Furthermore, Debbie has lived a meaningful life full of service.

Clara with Debbie as a wee one

What we experienced back then and

Debbie in the cattle trough by the old cow barn, Dad took her with him to feed.

continue to realize is when God is the center of our lives, even in troubled times, our character is strengthened. The family still praises God in the good times and the bad. Psalm 42:1 reads, "As the deer pants for water, so my soul pants for you, O God." True, we still pant for the way of God.

Crank Phones and Party Lines

Do you remember the old crank phones? Well, I do. Ours hung on the wall in the kitchen next to the back door. Our designated ring was one long and one short. Everyone on the party line had a designated ring consisting of longs and shorts. Around 1961, we got a rotary dial

An old crank phone just like ours

wall phone. We were excited for the modern phone. I recall our number was KEystone 7-2460.

Speaking of party lines, have you ever had a party line? Youngsters nowadays don't have a clue what that is. All they know are cell phones with their own unique numbers.

Back in the old days, we'd crank the phone to get assistance. The cranking made a sound to alert the operator. Sometimes, we lifted the earpiece and said, "Hello, Mae?" Mae Ray was the twenty-four-hour switchboard operator. Their home in Paragon had the actual switchboard in the house. My siblings and I have been in that home to see the switchboard. Though it was a small home, the switchboard was a replica like in the movies.

The Ray's—Mae, Guernsey, and their daughter Judy—lived in the home with the switchboard. Mae's daughter sometimes worked on the switchboard also. They assisted with calls in the night, if needed. During the day, other operators would fill in on occasion.

Recently, when a childhood neighbor, Henry, came home for a visit, he noticed all the *old* phone numbers listed on the inside his parents' old crank phone. His brother Ron still lives on their family farm, affectionately named "Springvale Farm." Fortunately, no one ever removed the names with all the scribbles. There it was— the complete list of the party-line names along with

Springvale Farm's Phone with the numbers
faintly written on the face.

Party Line.....The Original Social Media...

With some bright light and research, I re
farm. The Party Line rings were Longs a

AF Burnett. (1) 1 Short 1 Long
Harry Dow (3) 1 Long 1 Short
Melvin Dow (5) 1 Long 2 Shorts
Harold Finney (4) 2 Shorts 1 Long
Jesse Hill (7) 2 Longs 1 Short
Fount Johnson (12) 1 Long 3 Shorts
Sylvan Shuler (9) 1 Long 1 Short 1 Long
JB Whitaker ( ) 1 Short 1 Long 1 Short
Paragon Telephone Line

From Henry. This was our party line.

their designated rings. A sentimental find without a doubt.

This is how it worked on a party line with a crank phone. When the phone rang, it rang in everyone's home on that party line. Little by little, interested parties picked up and eavesdropped on the conversation. Soon someone would announce, "Everyone who is not supposed to be listening to this conversation, please hang up!" Then several clicks sounded off. Few phone calls were received back in those days. If a call was received, it was usually exciting news or a loved one calling from afar. Everyone was nosey.

George with Archie and Blanche on their front porch

Once, when George called while he was away in the navy, Dad picked me up to reach the phone, so I could talk with my brother. Currently, when I phone my other brother Philip to speak with his wife Patty, he always says, "Just a minute while I hold her up to the phone." He thinks he's funny.

Later, when Dad went out and left us alone at night, neighborhood friends came over. As kids do, we'd sometimes get into mischief. Now that we had a rotary dial phone, making a prank call was much easier.

We all made prank calls. I was about twelve and I dialed a neighbor lady, Cora Wigal. "Hello, is your refrigerator running?" I proudly asked. Cora replied, "Yes." To which I responded, "Well you'd better go catch it!" Then I slammed the phone down. (Kids today know nothing about the sheer delight of "slamming" the handset down on the cradle in the heat of excitement or anger. What a release that was back then.)

Anyway, secondly, I pranked Cora again saying, "Do you have Prince Albert in a can?" (Prince Albert is a brand of tobacco.) The reply was, "You'd better let him out before he suffocates." To my surprise, Cora Wigal promptly called our house. Upon answering the phone without caller ID, she confronted me.

"Phyllis Ann, what are you doing?" I was busted and never prank called anyone again. Truthfully, she was delighted to hear from me, and frankly, I was afraid of her. I didn't want her to tell my dad I was pranking people on the phone.

My friend Debbie M. saw my articles in the paper. She read them to her husband's ninety-four-year-old grandmother while visiting her in the nursing home. Grandma Betty, having a sharp mind, declared, "Hey, I grew up on 'Turkeyneck Hill' too. I know the Dow family and we were good neighbors."

Grandma continued, "We have the old crank phone from the Dow family." Well, that piqued my interest. I asked Debbie, "Where is the crank phone now?" Debbie asked Grandma Betty, and she thought one of her sons had it. After some inquiring by my sister Lois, the phone was found.

As it turned out, after our big house burned to the ground in 1956, Grandma Betty's dad loaned a crank phone to my dad. Several years later, after we got the new rotary wall phone, the old crank phone was used for a hat rack.

By and by, my dad finally returned the crank phone to its original owner, Avis and Chub, who lived on Arthur Road. Their daughter Linda had the phone last, Grandma Betty's youngest sister. Now they have all passed, and who knows where the phone hangs.

Isn't it amazing how simple memories surrounding a crank phone take on a life of their own?

Farm Deliveries and Pickups

Did you ever have delivery services like the Rawleigh or Fuller Brush man? One peddled antiseptic salve, and the other sold a selection of brushes out of his large case door-to-door. How about the bread man? I loved the bread man. He had donuts, and sometimes, Mom would get us a package of those delicious, powdered donuts. Of course, they'd be gone in a flash.

What about the milkman? Ours was the one who picked up our skimmed cream in those large milk cans. He was more of a pick up man because he never delivered anything to our home.

I remember a rather morbid *pick up* man. We called him the *dead animal man*. His job was to come to the farm with a special kind of truck to take the dead animal away. I am not sure where they went with the carcass. I will say if it took a day or so, those animals would swell up and legs sticking out. It was gross.

We even had the Farm Bureau Co-Op driver deliver gasoline to an elevated tank kept in our barnyard. We never went to the gas station to put gas in our family car, just to the barnyard. Often, it was too muddy for the car. We filled a gas can and carried it to the car parked near our house. Hopefully, the sloppy mud would dry up soon, so we could gas up in the barnyard. On today's farm, I don't think tractors use the same kind of fuel as our automobiles.

Besides getting our newspapers delivered, not much is home delivery any longer. Nowadays, we may have the Schwan man in rural areas. I've been known to flag down a Schwan truck on the road to buy ice cream and frozen foods.

What I liked best was when I was the only one home. Mom heard or saw the peddler's truck come in the driveway. During the summers when the doors and windows were open, we hid behind the heat stove when the guy knocked if Mom didn't want anything. She didn't want to be persuaded and hiding was her way of saying "No." I thought it was hilarious at the time, but she threatened, "Don't even breathe loud because he can hear us." What did I know? I was a kid, so I held my breath and was obedient to a fault. This was a memory all right. All I wanted were those white powdered donuts!

When the gasoline delivery man came, it was a real treat. It didn't matter what we were doing or where we were, all the kids ran to the gas man. His name was Verle Maxwell who hauled fuel for the Farm Bureau Co-Op. Verle was always nice, friendly, and spoke kindly to us the entire time he was pumping gasoline into our elevated farm tank.

We waited patiently while engaging in conversation. What we really wanted was what he always gave us just before he left the barnyard, a piece of hard candy. Verle always stashed a bag of either cinnamon balls, butterscotch, or star mints in a brown paper bag on the seat of his truck. Verle wanted to visit with us to hear of our day, and we wanted candy. What a smart man he was, and we never forgot him or his simple gesture. That was a happy childhood memory.

We were fortunate to be raised on the farm where we had all the pork and beef we wanted to eat. Sometimes, we didn't have a garden in the latter years. The older kids *got out of dodge* as soon as they graduated from high school. So, the laborers were fewer to tend a garden.

I remember one time when it was just me and Philip remaining on the farm. It was late summer when most gardens were full of vine ripened tomatoes. We had plenty of bacon or jowl bacon but no tomatoes. Philip drove the tractor to the Carters' home where they had a roadside produce stand. He bought a three-gallon bucket full of juicy ripe tomatoes. Philip held that bucket in one hand and drove the tractor with the other. He was so talented.

While Philip was gone, I got busy frying bacon for our bacon and tomato sandwiches. "Mmm, they were tasty." Of course, we had no lettuce, but we didn't need any. We didn't eat all the tomatoes, but we ate all the bacon. That is a dandy memory. I can almost taste the sandwich now as my mouth just watered. Or— maybe, I'm hungry.

Since we had chickens, we had eggs. Lots of eggs. We ate eggs every day. I remember making angel food cake and egg noodles. That way, we used the whole egg for those two recipes. Homemade angel food cake is delicious, and we all gobbled freshly made egg noodles. Our mom made noodles a lot, and then when Clara had her own home, she made them as well. Both were yummy.

Philip and I had the job of cleaning the eggs for the hatchery. These were fertile eggs and someday would be baby chicks. We used a sandpaper brush to rid the egg of any debris or chicken waste stuck on the egg. The brush was a foam-padded wooden block with a two-inch-wide piece of sandpaper fitted around the block. Brushing those eggs every Sunday evening was a dreaded job. Dad took them to the hatchery on Monday mornings. This was not a pleasant memory, but it needed to be done so Dad could make the delivery. We could have kept up with cleaning the eggs all week long, but since the job was not pleasant, we procrastinated.

In today's modern world, we do have delivery services, it's called Amazon, Grubhub, Instacart, as well as many other options. Everything is delivered, except we must go online to place the order. In fact, we never have to leave home to shop for anything these days.

Amazon is unlike the early days on the farm, no personal touches, no conversation, no powdered-sugar donuts, and no hard candy. Just lots of deliveries.

Thunder, Lightning, and Sunshine

Our farm always included livestock. My brother Philip and his wife Patty still raise cattle and goats on the family farm. We used cats to get rid of mice in the barns and storage sheds. The dogs were just pals to hang with while working around the farm. It amazed me how many times kittens were born. It also amazed me how darn cute kittens were, but they always grew into cats, who are not so cute to me.

Our family dog named "Mustard," unfortunately contracted rabies. In a few weeks, surprisingly, many of us were bitten by our gentle dog. Dad had the dog evaluated at the veterinarian clinic. Sadly enough, he was rabid and had to be put down.

Those of us bitten saw Dr. Eisenberg at his Martinsville office for fourteen days in a row. We each received rabies shots with a long needle surrounding our belly button. Ouch! This kept us from foaming at the mouth because we had rabies. It worked, but

Yours truly with Mustard and a lap pup

it might explain a lot of our crazy dispositions at times. This occurred in 1955.

Dogs and cats were never allowed in our house while growing up. The animals lived outside, and people lived inside.

We didn't think about it. Golly, how things have changed.

Another thing, we tried not to get too attached to any of our dogs. They chased cars and the cars always won. It was common to find our pooch dead in the road. Later, we'd find another dog. One dog we named Lucky. He was run over three times before he finally ran out of lives.

Onward to the 70s when my three daughters were still little stinkers. We lived in the city and never around animals. When the girls were near pets, they were frightened into a frenzy. We thought an Irish Setter pup would make them like dogs. The pup grew large rather quickly. When outdoors, she barked a lot. She broke collars and ran away. We tried a choker collar, but it wasn't long before the beautiful red setter was stolen.

Afterward, we acquired a blonde cocker spaniel puppy, Buckwheat. He chewed everything in sight. Before long, we found Buckwheat a delightful home who wanted a dog for their little boy. The lesson the girls learned is— dogs are cute and lovable, but they aren't going to live with us.

In the mid-90s, daughter Kitte moved in with me while she transitioned from an out-of-state job. One day, I came home, the door to the hall bathroom was closed. I knocked and no one answered. Suddenly, I heard a faint "meow. Sure enough, she had brought two kitten's home. I didn't want any kittens which grow into cats! But there they were.

Kitte got home from work, and I jokingly asked, "How soon are you moving?" She replied, "Aren't they the cutest little things, Mom?" By the weekend, they roamed the house.

On Friday night, I was lying on the couch watching TV. When Kitte came home from her night out, the kittens were curled up on my chest. I didn't feel them climb on me while I slept. Kitte was excited to see me with them, she said, "Mom, you've bonded with the kittens!" "Wrong!"

The next week, Kitte saw the *Lion King* movie. Since the kittens were not named, as Kitte arrived home, she picked up the tabby cat with her arms extended overhead and said, "Simba!" She named the other cat Sierra. Kitte and her cats moved a few months later.

In the early 2000s, Kitte had a precious Maltese dog named Lucy until she passed at age fourteen. Katte's handsome Welsh-Terrier dog is named Huxley. My third daughter, Jessica, has absolutely no use for any pet unless it's a rock. Jessi is a lot like her mother.

When I lived in the country in Scottsburg, IN, an elderly couple had three little kittens. One May, they offered me one. Not being a pet person, I said, "I'll take all three but not one, kittens need friends. I live alone and not at home much. I don't want to be their only friend."

The three kittens came home with me. The bright yellow tabby cat I named Sunshine. Then the swift tan and white one,

Sunshine, Lightning, and Thunder was meowing as usual

who was a scaredy-cat, Lightning. The last one Thunder for he was a talkative feline always starving for attention. His breed was a calico and black tabby.

They were content until Sunshine was run over by a car. Later, Lightning was murdered by coyotes during the winter solstice. Thunder became depressed from witnessing a murder. I felt bad because he needed Prozac or a new home. He moved to a new home with children and other cats.

Beautiful Thunder with his full winter coat

My three cats were a delight for eight months, but as they say, "Like all good things, they must come to an end."

The Wormhole Plate

Every family has a story or two of situations which happened at mealtime. Ours was no different. Growing up on a livestock farm, we always had plenty of meat at meals. Having a big garden meant we had lots of vegetables. Of course, much work was required to take care of those animals and the garden. But what else did we have to do?

We always had an abundance of labor but truly little free time. Most days, we spent all our time on the farm. One sure thing we learned from farming, we didn't want to work like that for the rest of our lives. Well, one brother does, but I won't mention any names, but his name starts with a P and ends with a P. I'm not saying who, though.

When I was a little girl, I wanted yellow mustard as my garnish for a piece of meat. The jar had never been opened, and I couldn't open it. I handed it to my brother George, and he couldn't open it, either. Dad tried next. He made a valiant effort then shook his head saying, "I can't get this lid off, could you try it again?" I did and it came off. Little did I know that Dad loosened the lid and allowed me to be the proud one who opened the mustard jar.

One year at the state fair, Dad got a sample of Lawry's Seasoned Salt. The kids didn't care for the taste at all. However, Dad loved it and sprinkled it on everything on his plate. He wouldn't start the meal unless it was on the table. Also, when Dad sat at the table, he sat with his feet to his right side. His feet were never under the table. We thought he was ready to get up in a hurry.

Like most people who plant a garden, they are anxious for the first harvest. Those foods include lettuce, radishes, onions, and the like. My mom made a delicious recipe for "wilted lettuce." It was leaf lettuce with onions and some bacon in a large bowl. The bowl needed to be large enough to serve several helpings once the lettuce had been wilted. The tasty dressing was made with bacon grease, vinegar, sugar, and water. Pour the boiling dressing over the bowl of lettuce, stir it up, and the lettuce shrinks to "wilted." Yum!

With eight in the family, we went through a lot of dishes. This was before Corelle and melamine. One of our china plates had cracked, and a small hole chipped out but was not broken all the way, so we still used it. It had a dark stain in the hole chip. One day, Lois had that plate. Unfortunately, her wilted lettuce included a worm from the garden. When she saw the worm, she swore it crawled out of the hole in the plate. From then on, no one wanted that plate, "the worm hole plate."

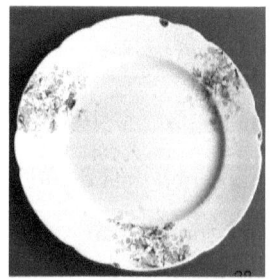

The wormhole plate.

Since we owned a milk cow, we had all the milk we wanted to drink. Sometimes, we made butter. This milk was not pasteurized nor was it homogenized. Louis Pasteur invented a way to kill the bacteria associated with milk, a process called pasteurization. Homogenization breaks down the fat to keep the milk from separating. Raw milk naturally allows the cream to rise to the top and the cream is the richest part of the milk. So, the

The big creamery can.

term, "the cream rises to the top" or other such sayings come from this process. Once a week, the milkman came by for the cream. We poured the skimmed cream which we had gathered all week long.

The fresh skimmed cream was a treat to add to our dry cereal. Because the milk was not pasteurized, it soured in a few days. Carol, a youngster, after tasting her spoiled milk claimed, "That doesn't taste very good," as she barely brushed her glass with the back of her little hand. The glass went over and spilled everywhere. You know what they say about spilled milk, you can't cry over it, but she did.

Philip was a shy young lad as he stuck his little hand around the bowl in front of him. He said, pointing his index finger in a curve, "I want some of that over there." Some remember he also spilled his milk doing that, but I don't. I just remember the story of his crooked finger being repeated often.

Frequently, we set our meat out of the freezer to defrost. One day someone sat out two chickens. They were unwrapped and sitting on the countertop. We didn't have a screen in the back door, so the main door always had to be closed. At age thirteen, I came running in the house busting to use the bathroom. No one else was inside, and I didn't shut the door like I should have. After my bathroom break, I went to my room before returning to the kitchen. To my surprise, there were two barn cats hunkered over those two thawing chickens. They were licking and biting into that chicken about to have a feast, all while glaring at me. It was hard to chase them out of the house as they were hungry. I didn't tell anyone about the cats for fear I would be in trouble for not shutting the door. At dinner, I didn't eat any chicken, only vegetables. Seems I was not hungry for chicken that night.

The best memory regarding those mealtime stories was the love and the closeness we felt for each other as a family.

Sibling Birthday Celebrations

It has been said, "wedding cake can cause a bride to gain weight." I say, "so does birthday cake." Of course, what is a celebration without cake? Life is too short to be cake-less, so put your fork in hand and be ready!

In the late 1980s, my siblings and I started meeting for birthday lunches. Since we were all working, we met centrally so we'd get back to work in a timely fashion. George worked and lived in Florida and couldn't join the fun until 1995 when he moved to Indiana. Carol drove a school bus, and I sold insurance. The rest worked near each other in Indianapolis. Our retired Aunt Bessie enjoyed sharing the birthday luncheons with us as well.

After we retired, it has become a dinner or lunch celebration or a day outing for the birthday. The party often includes other kin and friends. We always love having more people along. Although my siblings and I don't agree on everything, our relationship takes priority over disagreement.

Clara enjoying another birthday

Since our parents divorced while in our youth, it became our intention to cherish one another. We understand this mutual sibling endearment is uncommon in our world today. Most of our friends do not cleave to their family of origin although some would like to. Our family is happy to make each birthday special for each one. I especially love the one shared in January.

Clara is the first born in our sibling line up, so let's start with her. March is her birth month with possible pleasant spring weather. However, it was often blustery on her birthday. Though Clara has left us for heaven, we still remember her on her birthday.

In birth order at a party. R to L Clara, George, Lois, Carol, Philip, Phyllis

Then two years and two months later, George arrived in May. He is the second in line of the siblings. May is a beautiful month with green grass to mow and flowers in bloom. Often idyllic weather abounds to enjoy the outdoors for his birthday.

George and Lois celebrating together

Lois followed two years later, still in the month of May. Not wanting to forget what month Lois was born, Mom named her Lois May. Though she is the smallest in stature of all of us, she was the biggest at birth. Poor Mom, A ten pounder.

Two months later is July. That was the month we celebrated Aunt Bessie's birthday. In 2010, sixteen of us went to dinner. After dinner we were at my home for birthday cake, desserts, and visiting. Aunt Bessie was still in her party clothes reclining in her easy chair the next morning. The Lord called her home at age eighty-nine. She partied with her loved ones for her birthday, then left. What a way to go! We still miss her.

Nowadays, in the month of July we go to the Morgan County fair and see all the "Dow" projects. In addition, we usually watch some goat and swine shows. That is a long-held tradition to attend the county fair.

September, two years later, Mom has Carol making the scene. It is the time for fall harvest and honeybees. We all enjoy the colors and aromas of fall, our favorite season. Carol is the fourth in line of the siblings.

Just in time for putting things away for the winter, along came Philip. He came swooping out in November, two years and two months away from September. It is amazing how this all works. A birth every two years and a celebration every two months.

At Christmas, we always get together with the whole Dow clan. Gathering the whole family is a big treat for the six siblings. We keep adding to our numbers in the Dow family. All the grandchildren are having babies now. We have well over 110 family members as of this writing in 2022. This includes the in-laws as well. They are part of the family.

Of course, the sixth and last sibling is yours truly, Phyllis. I am quite sure Mom and Dad saved the best for last. Being born in

January, two years and two months from Philip makes the cycle complete.

Clara is the top of the birth order, and I am the bottom. The cycle is in perfect birth order and every two months we have a celebration. God couldn't have planned it better. So, we have Clara, George, Lois, Carol, Philip, and me. Quite a crowd.

My birthday is January 10. Our ages are all in the same decade for a year, and then a new decade starts again. It happens that way every ten years.

When I turned seventy, I received a sweatshirt that says on the front, "I have survived the 60's twice." It was given to me by my hairdresser, Debi Owens. Think about it for a moment! When I wear it, many people point and strike up a conversation. I am all too eager to talk about the sweatshirt and the saying.

The only photo of our whole family together. The rest burned in the house fire.

Many of us don't have just one birthday celebration, but several with many friends. If any of you want to get in on them, let me know. I like cake, and I'll have my "fork up," ready, and waiting.

As far as life on the farm goes, we didn't realize how fortunate we were with the bounty of food served at every meal. Though we shared plenty of heartache and loss, we were blessed and fed in many ways.

Manure In Springtime

Growing up on the farm with my five siblings was never dull. Our Dad's idea of discipline was to keep us busy working, and we wouldn't have time to squabble with one another. Little did he know we found the time. One thing for sure, there was always an abundance of work to do, even if we didn't want to do it.

Every season had plenty of jobs that needed to be completed. Springtime, the fields needed to be plowed and prepared for planting. Once the planting was complete, the hay fields were tall enough to cut, so we baled the hay. Sometimes we baled hay two or three cuttings per summer. That was a sweaty job, and usually involved hiring temporary farm hands. Having a lot of other people on the farm felt like a party even though it was a lot of work.

Often, we walked through the soybean fields to pull up corn that was growing in the middle of the soybeans. Not fun. My sister Lois figured if a farmer had corn growing in his soybean field, he didn't have any kids. Occasionally, we walked between the rows in corn fields to remove the tassels for pollination control. I never remembered doing that, but I heard about it.

In the winter, we helped cut fallen trees or limbs, split the big pieces, and haul the firewood back to the house. We had an opening to the basement where the wood burning furnace sat. It was called a "coal chute" but we rarely used coal.

We managed the livestock by sorting and moving the hogs and cattle from this barn or field to another. Every few months or at least a few times per year, we took a load to the stockyards. Payday needed to come along sooner or later.

Every day, we had chores to do, which involved feeding and watering all the animals. Every day. Even Christmas and our birthday. Even if you had a friend over. Those penned-up animals wanted to eat and drink, too.

But the worst job I remember was cleaning out the barns and sheds every late winter or early spring. We had beef cattle, hogs, and chickens who came inside when the weather was bad. Getting rid of the manure, for me, was a dreaded but necessary job. A job I didn't want any part of at all, yet we all had to do it.

Dad usually hired a neighboring farmer who had a tractor with a front-end loader to get the bulk of the waste cleaned up. Then Dad and my brother used a pitchfork around all the edges to get the manure out, and the barn cleaned up for spring. The chicken house was always done totally by hand, and that was the smelliest manure. Chicken manure is very aromatic. I sometimes helped when there was no one else to shovel. Being the youngest, a "no one else" time came soon enough.

Dad and brothers Philip or George spread the manure with a tractor pulling the spreader over the fields before we plowed, using it as extra fertilizer. They even spread manure on our garden plot. Have you heard that old saying, "You are what you eat?" Well, think about it.

Philip working on a tractor near the pole barn

Everything on the farm had a purpose and was used for something else. Nothing was wasted. We recycled about everything before it was a "green thing." This particular year, Dad had a young man come who was working for the neighbor farmer who owned the front-end loader. It just so happened, this young man was doing an internship at Samaria Baptist, our country church. We knew him, and he was a likable guy who liked to sing. And sing he did. He sang all the time whether anyone wanted to hear him or not. The noisy tractor's workings did well to drown out his singing. He was just singing his heart out while he scooped the manure into the spreader.

At this time, I was too young to be of any use for the task at

A manure spreader like the one we had.

hand. I was in the hay loft about twenty feet up, overlooking the area where they were working that day. For some reason, I had a softball with me and wanted to play. Instead of playing softball with my brother, I was hiding out in the loft to watch the buzz of activity below.

Suddenly, I heard the young man on the tractor sing out, "Drop the ball on his head" in a beautiful melody. Leaning over the edge, I looked down. There was Philip, my sweet brother, directly below where I was hiding out. The guy sang it out one more time, "Drop the ball on his head!" I shook my head no. Although I was tickled at the whole idea, I just could not do it. However, he was relentless with his instructional singing and kept nodding his head 'yes' as he sang. So, reluctantly, I dropped the ball, and it landed on my brother's head.

Poor Philip, he didn't know what hit him until he saw the softball on the ground. Springtime of long ago while cleaning out the barns, could be amusing.

City Cousins and Cigarettes

Back in the 1950s, life on a working farm was quite different from living in the city. For example, if one lives in the country yet they don't farm anything, raise anything, or grow anything, it is about the same as city life except they usually have more open space than city living. Of course, the cities and towns in rural communities have a small-town feel, unlike Indianapolis or Chicago.

When I was young, our city cousins Wyatt and Zane came to

Wyatt and Zane

visit us from the big town of Gosport. As most of you know, Gosport is a small municipality. However, the advantage for them was, they could walk to the store or post office, and we could not. Nevertheless, we affectionately called our cousins, "city slickers" because they didn't know the way of farm life. Of course, we didn't know the way of the city, but that didn't matter as they were on our turf. They usually came during the summer or Christmas break. In fact, they thought coming to the farm for a vacation was fun. So, we worked them to death doing our chores.

We put them to work carrying big gunnysacks of feed from one barn to the other, toting a five-gallon bucket of water to the hogs, or pitching silage down the silo. They would do it enthusiastically. The city cousins loved the challenge, we got to boss them around and watch. We were all happy. I recall a lot of laughter and fun when we were together.

If we were lucky in the winter, we had snow when the cousins visited. We were all too eager to put them on a piece of tin with the front bent up and send them down the big hill toward the creek bottom. The only instruction we gave them was to roll off it they were headed for a tree or a ravine. It's possible we were a little mischievous toward our naïve cousins. However, no permanent injuries were ever verified.

Our Grandma Stierwalt, Mom's mother, in front of the tower

A couple of times in the summer, I went to spend a few days at their home in Gosport. I remember walking from their home to my Grandma Stierwalt's home next to the water tower. She always had biscuits and jelly for a snack. That was amusing to freely roam the town. In the center of town was a park with a gazebo. We entertained

The Gosport gazebo where we played as kids

ourselves by pretending we were in a play. (We found out recently the Dow ancestry through our Grandma Dow is related to Ephraim Goss who founded the small town of Gosport in 1829.)

On one such occasion when fourteen-year-old cousin Wyatt was visiting the farm, he was primed to discover a variety of new experiences in life. For example, my dad kept his carton of cigarettes on top of the refrigerator in the kitchen. If neighbors came by and want cigarettes, he'd sell them a pack for a quarter. Which would save them from having to drive four miles to Paragon. Curious Wyatt wanted to experience smoking. There were lots of cigarette butts in the ash trays, but he wanted to try a fresh one. In fact, I even tried the cigarette butts back then. I'd light one up in front of the bathroom mirror to see how cool I looked and would even try to blow smoke rings. I found out I was not very cool, mostly I choked on the smoke. I never did start smoking and so glad I did not. Unfortunately, our dad died from acute emphysema when he was sixty-three. He smoked unfiltered cigarettes since he was sixteen years old.

Anyway, it took a lot of persuasion, but Wyatt talked my sister, Carol, into getting a pack of cigarettes, and they would merely place a quarter on top of the refrigerator. Then my dad would not be the wiser. We thought. Wyatt must have had the quarter because we never had any money. Consequently, he took the cigarettes and smoked a few, then took the rest home with him to Gosport. Carol didn't smoke with Wyatt because she was afraid of getting into trouble. Smart girl!

When Dad finally came in the house from working on the farm, he noticed a pack of cigarettes were missing. It was always extremely hard to get anything past him. Dad said, "Who has been messing with my cigarettes?" We never knew before that day he kept such good track of them. Carol indicated, "The neighbor came over to get a pack, and he left his quarter on the refrigerator." Dad said, "What does he think this is, a grocery store?" I still laugh about that when remembering my city cousins and cigarettes.

Ironically, when I left the farm, I became an urban dweller, and my girls became city slickers! Isn't it funny how being "all in" for country life can change to the city during a lifetime?

Teenage Boys and the Shootout

In the summer of 1956, my brother George was a teenager. Those of you who knew him then and know him now, not a lot has changed. Maybe his speed and stamina have slowed a bit, but his hankering for excitement has not.

He tells me many stories, and bless his heart, I write them down for the world to see. We attend insurance training seminars together and spend a fair amount of time looking through the windshield. This is a story I heard this week. It is probably true, but who knows. I know it was entertaining to me as we shared stories that day.

As teenage farm boys do, they go to town on weekends when all the chores are completed. One such time, brother George, Jim W., and Larry S. were hanging out in Paragon. They'd go to the Root Beer Stand and cruise the gas station restaurant where all the truckers stopped.

George, on the right, and his friends as a junior at Eminence High School

That restaurant had all sorts of truckers stopping to eat day and night. This was the route from Vincennes to Indianapolis along State Road 67. The Vincennes area used to grow delicious watermelon and muskmelon. With the mounded-up railroad tracks running parallel to SR 67, it provided a perfect cover for melon thieves. Not saying brother George partook of such larceny, but… the conditions were right.

Anyway, once the sidewalks were all rolled up about 2 a.m. in Paragon, they decided to head for home. Larry drove his dad's new pickup truck. They had the new license plate, but it was in the cab of the truck, not tagged.

The Paragon Town Marshal, Tom, and his deputy, D.S., cruised the town to make sure young boys stayed out of trouble. They were doing their duty. Of course, these three hooligans tried desperately to avoid the eye of the marshal and his trusty deputy.

The law usually parked by the water tower at the west edge of town. From that vantage point, they surveyed the traffic easily. Normally, the boys used this route when heading home. However, this night, the scrutiny of the town marshal and his side kick seemed unsettling to the boys because the plates were not tagged on the new truck yet.

Smith Street led north out of Paragon which connected with Graveyard Road. The three teenagers chose this longer way home. To their surprise, the marshal and deputy were sitting in an unmarked car just off Smith Street and took after them at the north edge of town. A chase ensued.

I asked George, "Why did you run?" He said, "Larry said he would be in big trouble if his dad found out he had not tagged the plate to the truck. Not only that, but we also weren't positive that it was the law that was chasing us."

They approached the ninety-degree turn going north bound at Graveyard and Smith with such speed, Larry ran through the stop sign. The home near this intersection is where Tom, the marshal, lived. He flew past the stop sign without stopping as well!

These were all one-lane gravel roads at the time. Hot and dry summer weather created a dust cloud billowing behind the teenage boys, the lead vehicle. The heavy dust ballooned over the second vehicle in hot pursuit, the law. The makeshift red light was shining, yet the boys couldn't see it nor were they slowing down.

Graveyard Road ran along the hill line on a flat curvy road. Since the boys were not stopping, the deputy decided to pull a Barney Fife. He reared his upper body out of the window and started shooting at the back tires. The boys thought they were firing at them personally. So, Larry sped up, going as fast as he could.

When the pickup reached Strawberry Lane and turned right, they heard it. A thump, thump—thump, thump. They had a flat tire and had to stop. The right rear tire had been shot and killed.

Of course, the three scared-half-to-death teenagers surrendered. Still Tom, the town marshal and "Barney" walked up to them with their guns still pulled. They piled the boys in the back of the unmarked car for a ride to town.

After questioning, the only one held was Larry. They carted him off to jail in Martinsville and cut George and Jim loose in Paragon. It was now 3 a.m., and George wasn't about to call home for a ride. He had to walk four miles home, while poor Jim had to mosey on another two miles to his home.

George sitting on a teachers lap on a dare one year at Eminence High

Funny how some things never change on hot summer nights among the teenage boy population. If mothers only knew the truth of their darling little angels.

Developing Understandings

The Night Our Old Barn Burned

Most people have never lived through the trauma of losing their home to a fire. That is good news. As a family, we not only lost our huge multi-generational farmhouse, but we also lost one of two massive barns on the farm to a fire.

In August 1956, we lost our family home and spent a few weeks in an old garage, a carriage house. It had been converted into a storage bin for grain and farm tools. A few weeks later our family moved to the little three-room Grandpa Goss home at the top of Turkeyneck Hill.

The old carriage house where we lived after the house burned. Another big Duroc hog.

Time passed, and the new construction of the ranch home was nearing completion where the "Big house" had stood. Every night, we completed the regular chores in the barnyard before driving back over to the Grandpa Goss house. Chores like feeding and watering the penned-up livestock, milking the cow, and gathering the eggs.

George recalled as a youngster when he did the chores by carrying a lantern for light, especially in the winter months when the sun didn't shine very many hours per day. It was a major upgrade when they installed electricity in every building of the barnyard. George said, "It was impressive to flip a switch, and the whole barn lit up. Even at the old cow barn near the west field with the attached silo, Dad installed a big lamp at the top which illuminated the whole area. That was a significant help."

The large white barn nearest the home appeared like something in a Norman Rockwell painting. The barn had a driveway through the center. The passageway is where we pulled the wagons of hay to offload into the lofts. The lofts reached to the roof line on both sides. Installed near the center of the roof was a track with ropes, pulleys, and hooks to load and unload hay and straw. The alleyway was long enough to park the stock truck as well as a tractor at the same time; or even a wagonload hitched to a tractor. It was convenient to pull farm implements out of the weather.

The big white barn on the right, taken from the roof of the house.

Our barn yard in July 1956 displaying all the barns. Including the other big cow barn with a silo.

Consequently, both the front and the rear of the barn had large sliding doors on tracks. They also had smaller sliding doors to allow livestock to enter/exit, among other doors to access. The attached silo led to a walkway between feeding troughs. That very walkway is where Lois was running from George and her leg was torn open by a protruding bolt from the trough.

Stories are told of our horses, but I never remember having a horse on the farm. I often daydreamed of having a pony and even rode a stick horse around the barnyard. At the west end of the barn were horse stalls. In my day, Dad used those to store feed and tools, never horses.

The exterior was painted a bright white. The post and beam construction were solid wood with joints adhering by wooden pegs. We all believe the majestic barn would still be standing today had it not burned. That old barn had character and we loved it.

In the early spring of 1958, George walked from milking the cow in another barn. He remembers, "As I passed in front of the big white barn, I saw a flicker of light through the front window. I placed the milk bucket in the car, then went to check out the light switch. The lights to the barn were off."

He continued, "I entered the barn and noticed the hayloft over the horse stalls was on fire. The Farmall H tractor was in the barn with the corn picker attached. I was able to drive the 'H' out quickly."

"The truck full of corn had a tarp covering the bed and was in the barn as well. Woefully, the truck would not start. So, I got the other tractor, the F-20, opened the back barn door, and pulled the truck out of the burning barn."

In the pasture behind the barn was a big mud hole or a small pond. It gathered rain as it ran down from the barnyards. George said, "The side boards of the truck were already burning, but I pulled that truck to that pond with the tractor. Then I used buckets to splash water on the truck to extinguish the fire.

"In the meantime, someone called the fire department in Paragon four miles away," George said. "I remember my friend Gary was there, and he got all the cattle out from the other side."

By the time the fire department arrived, it was too late. The barn was burnt to the ground, but all the big tools, implements, and livestock were saved thanks to George's quick action. Our poor parents. They lost their big house and their big barn in less than two years. Without a doubt, the stress of the immense losses weighed heavy on Mom and Dad. In the fall of 1958, they were separated and then divorced.

At this time, Clara was married and was expecting number two. George joined the navy right after graduation a few months later. The rest of us remained on the farm to help Dad and continue the stability of the life we had there. Yes, it was a sad time for all, but we managed to make life tolerable and survived without Mom. Being the youngest, it felt empty. Our dad was forty years old, and Mom was only thirty-six.

A pole barn was built where the picturesque barn once stood, but nothing could ever replace the beautiful memories. Our grandpa Charlie Dow built memories for some of the older siblings working around that "barn of character." Apparently, the faulty wiring was the culprit, again.

The silver lining was the truck, tractor, and other equipment were saved. All the livestock was moved out of harm's way, as well. We must count our blessings and name them one by one, especially during a tragedy such as this.

During times of loss, we often search in the scriptures to find solace in our suffering. These are some. Psalm 30:5 tells us, "… his favor lasts a lifetime; weeping may stay for the night, but **joy** comes in the morning."

1 Thessalonians 4:13 reads, "…do not grieve like the rest of mankind who have no hope."

Jeremiah 29:11 states, "For I know the plans I have for you," declares the Lord, "plans to prosper you and not to harm you, plans to give you hope and a future."

Somehow, we rested, revived, and renewed our hope and joy.

Coon Hunting in the Hollers

Have you ever been raccoon hunting? (In the country they call them *coon* instead of raccoon.) The sport of *coon huntin'* is not intended for the physically weak. My dad was an avid coon hunter. A few of his offspring have hunted with him; for me it was a one and done.

The history of coon hunting dates to early Native Americans times. However, "scent hounds" were imported to America from Europe. Basically, these hounds instinctively follow the scent and trail the raccoon. Once treed, they howl in a way that tells their master, "Come hither and get this varmint."

During the hunt, the hunter follows the coon dog as he howls and barks when he has caught the scent. The dog chases the prey through the woods. While in hot pursuit of the raccoon, many hills and hollers may be crossed. Once the dog wails he has treed a coon, the hunter scurries to the tree which could be a few hundred yards away, or further.

I was fascinated how coon dogs were not interested in a dead coon; they loved the chase of the live ones. Dad reasoned coon hounds are sporting animals and not pets. Their job was to tree coons, and the hunter didn't want any distractions. True, the coon dog was as equally important as the rifle.

Let's talk about coon hounds. There are special breeds whose instincts are to run and chase which is perfect for chasing coons up a tree. These short-haired long-legged dogs are gentle in spirit and great with kids.

The most popular is Bluetick. They go back to the early 1900s and come from Louisiana. The Bluetick is black and white with blue speckles mixed in the white hair. The biggest coon dog is the black and tan with their lineage going back to eleventh century England. Of course, their coats are black and tan.

A deep golden dog breed, Redbone was another coonhound. We had one named Mustard. Unfortunately, he contracted rabies and bit most of us. We got rabies shots and unfortunately, Mustard was put down. Of all his dogs, his Bluetick, "Smokey," helped Dad win numerous awards and trophies at the Quincy Conservation Club.

The hunt begins after dark when the raccoons are on the move. One night, when my brother, Philip, was about eight years old, he followed Dad on a hunt. The dogs led them over Turkeyneck Hill and ended up on Graveyard Road in the bottoms, about three miles away from home.

As the hunt continued up Mannan Hill, Philip stopped Dad. "We have bagged three coons, it's past midnight, could I wake up Roy Hill and have him take me home?" Dad replied, "No, come on with me."

They finished the hunt and Philip was a tired little boy. What made it difficult for Philip, Dad had only one flashlight. Going through the woods, Dad released the branches and bushes while blazing a trail. If Philip stayed too close, the branches and bushes could whack him in the face. Otherwise, he was stumbling in the dark, trying to keep up. Poor little fella.

Dad sold the raccoon pelts. The carcasses were given to someone who enjoyed the delicacy of raccoon on their palate.

Dad with his trophy, pelts, and Smokey

When Philip left the navy, he, his wife, Patty, and their children lived with Dad for a while. Frequently, Patty grabbed some beef or pork from the basement freezer. At times, she was startled by an entire coon laying in the freezer staring back at her. Dad had gutted them and would skin them later.

Philip and Patty's daughter, Tami, was about seven when she was petting and feeding one of Dad's coon dogs named Josephine. Dad saw his little granddaughter with the dog and told her, "Tami, get away from that

Tami was a perky little girl back then and still is today

dog, she is not a pet!" Little Tami replied, "She was smiling at me, so I gave her some food. I think she likes me." Dad was not happy.

One night in my early teens, Dad woke me in the wee hours to run to Paragon for rifle shells. His trusty Bluetick treed a coon, and Dad ran out of ammunition.

I pleaded, "The hardware is closed." Dad told me, "Go to Teddy Bear Marsh's home, wake him up, and tell him what I need." Dad was emphatic. I drove to town (without a driver's license) and pounded on Teddy Bear's door. He retrieved the shells, and I delivered them to Dad in the woods. Mercy me.

During the peak of coon season in the late 1970s, 5.2 million raccoons were bagged in one season. The coon hunting season in Indiana is November 8 to January 31. So, if this is of interest you in the least, get your walking boots on, because this is not a sissy hike. You will be scurrying like a man on a mission. Hope your endurance is built up.

What motivated Dad not only were the trophies but selling the pelts. During the depression people used raccoons for food and sold the pelts to furriers. Hunters still sell the pelts.

Philip sometimes delivered coon meat to buyers at his work in Allisons. One condition, Dad had to leave at least one paw on the carcass to identify it was a coon. Yikes! I suppose that ensures it is what they say it is. I suppose it could have been a ground hog.

Whether you have ever coon hunted or not, it is a great sport primarily between a dog and his master. My dad had a great friend and companion with his prize dog named Smokey.

When Dad Kicked the Rooster

The first time my dad ever took an airplane ride was when my twins were born. At age fifty-one, he waited for a memorial event to ever board a plane. In February 1970, Dad received the call I was in labor.

Unbeknownst to me, Dad had asked my husband to call him the moment I went to the hospital to deliver. While in the recovery room, Dad came to my bedside to surprise me. Since I was the youngest, there had already been thirteen grandchildren born to my siblings. He was eager to fly to Pittsburgh to see me and his newborn twin granddaughters. My twins made him fifteen grandchildren. He always wanted a large family, and we were getting large.

That was the kind of man my dad was.

Every parent has shortcomings regardless of how much they try to do the right things. My dad was no different. Dad did something he never wanted to do before; he flew from Indianapolis for my big day. That kind gesture meant the world to me.

Personally, I have vivid memories the day they were born at St. Francis Hospital in *Pittsburgh*. Of course, this was when we waited until birth to know the gender of your baby. No ultrasound imaging was offered. I was so large at six months; my doctor ordered an X-ray. The news came on the Wednesday before Thanksgiving 1969. Sure enough, I was carrying two fetuses, twins.

Here are more tales regarding our dad and his character. This happened several years before the happy *red-letter* day of the birth of my twins. Tag along as I recall the details.

Circumstances were unclear to me then; our mother left the farm when I was nine years old. My oldest sister Clara was already married, and my oldest brother George was serving in the navy. So, there we were, the remaining four siblings. We lived on the farm on Turkeyneck Hill Road with our dad in charge of everything. Our dad was only forty years old at the time of the divorce. Looking back, it seems like a desperate time, but I didn't notice any hardship. It was like old times only without Mom there to look after us. The older siblings took care of the house and many things that Mom always did in Mom's absence. Everyone looked after me.

The best way Dad knew to raise us kids was to have us working on the farm and keeping us busy. This ultimately taught us many life lessons. We toiled in every facet of farming. The truth is these were the best learning experiences any kid could have. The wisdom we gained about life, crops, animal care, and daily living were understood by doing. Not only that, but we were also assured to have many *teachable* moments. Sometimes those *moments* were not pleasant but rarely repeated.

We observed our dad as he interacted with the livestock. The cattle, hogs, chickens, and dogs all knew who their master was. Not so much with my siblings and me. The animals sensed we were kids and didn't demonstrate authority like our dad.

I was not very brave. When large cows came near me, I went the other way, especially when I was young. The same was true of hogs. I didn't go near the adult males, *the boars*. They scared me to death with their frothing jowls when the sows were around. *What was that all about?*

Often Dad walked around in an enclosed lot with any of his livestock anytime. He held dominion over the animals of the farm. He *was* the master, and they knew he was the boss. First, with stubborn animals, he would sometimes need to use force. Second, when loading cattle and hogs into the truck, he occasionally needed to use an electric shocker to goose them along.

The large Duroc breed of boar hogs could be difficult to manage. With them, Dad used a *driving board,* a large board about three feet long and two feet tall with a handle. He carried the board between him and the boar. In his other hand, he held a four-foot whip. Dad was able to move them where he wanted.

The roosters tried to flog us and sometimes did. They were very territorial when they felt threatened. Who knew what their problem was. If you haven't been flogged, it is not fun. Not only that, but the sneaky roosters also scare you to pieces by their frightening demeanor.

Flogging by a rooster is an act of protecting his hens and territory. He charges swiftly with his head lowered, and when reaching his target, he not only flaps his wings, but attacks with clawed feet and spurs on the inside of his legs. He aggressively pecks and bites his adversary. When you see two or more roosters having what seems like a barnyard brawl, they are deciding the *pecking* order or *cock of the walk*.

When I was about six years old, I followed my dad around the barnyard doing chores. Out of nowhere, the rooster came charging toward my dad and struck his legs. Turning around

A happy rooster

quickly, Dad squarely kicked that rooster. The bird tumbled in the air like a soccer ball for about twenty yards. When he landed, my dad was charging after him. From that day forward, the rooster ran away from Dad when he was in the barnyard.

Recalling this story, kicking the rooster has a new meaning to me. Our dad was fearless, and his self-confidence gave each of his children the security and model to survive in this world. Sadly, we lost Dad at age sixty-three in July 1982. His life lessons took root in all his children, even though he was extremely strict. Maybe his strictness was the reason we have all done well in life.

One day I asked Dad, "Did you intend on having six children or were the last few an accident." His response was a quote from the Bible. Psalm 127:4,5 tells us, "Like arrows in the hands of a warrior are children born in one's youth. Blessed is the man whose quiver is full of them…" I think Dad would have had six more if Mom was willing. It always amazed me how much of the Bible he quoted, but he rarely attended church. His parents and grandparents were all very devout Christians.

As our lives continue—we still miss him every day, even though Dad was known to make a rooster fly.

Intern Preachers and Farm Life

For some reason, we often had a summer intern preacher working on our farm when I was a little kid. He would happily sing hymns while he toiled. If we knew the songs, we'd sing along.

One bright sunny day, I was in the bed of the stock truck with the intern while he was putting up the stock racks. Per usual, he was singing. He asked me, "What will your dad haul, cattle or hogs." I told him, "A load of hogs for the market, taking them to the stockyards."

Dad in a wagon with the stock truck in the background

For those of you who do not know, a stockyard is the place farmers take their animals to sell. There, the animals are sold to meat packers for butchering. The packers have their own slaughtering plants to pack the meat. They'd sell to wholesalers who in turn sold to retailers. That's the cycle of how you get your bacon, steak, pork chops, etc.

I was privileged to go with Dad to the stockyards on more than one occasion. What a site, grizzly guys in bib overalls smoking cigars there to bid on the livestock for the packers. They stood with one foot on the bottom fence board while leaning with their elbows on the top board. The aroma of livestock might stink on the ground, but it smells like money to everyone but me.

The animals are weighed and sorted by gender and age. After getting a ticket from the intake clerk showing the bill of sale, we walked to the office to get paid. Near the office, there was a restaurant which always served delicious vegetable beef soup. Dad treated us to soup for lunch. Driving home, Dad sometimes pulled the truck over at *Biff's Bakery* in Mooresville to buy a bag of glazed donuts. Life couldn't get much better than that. At least that is what ran through my mind.

Anyway, the young preacher asked, "What breed are the hogs?" "Durocs," I replied. Before long, he was singing, "I've got a home in glory land that outshines the sun." He sang that verse three times ending with, "look away beyond the blue." Then he loudly sang, "Oh Duroc, oh Duroc, oh do remember me; oh Duroc, oh Duroc, oh do remember me. Look away beyond the blue."

My little five-year-old mind knew those were not the words to that song I had sang in church, so I firmly stated, "It's not oh Duroc! It's Oh Do Lord!" He laughed because he knew the correct words.

Our dad's many friends often raised the same breeds of livestock as he did. Occasionally, growers came to our farm for gatherings. The farmers shared information pertinent to animal husbandry as well as field crops. Many returned to our farm in the spring to go mushroom hunting.

Regardless of the reason they visited, they usually joined us for a meal. It was common to have extras at our table. The farmers of that day were very friendly and generous. I suppose that chivalrous attitude remains intact today.

One time, I was at the bathroom sink with one of the men while washing our hands. He said, "Friends who wash and wipe together are good friends forever." What an inclusive and kind gesture he extended to a child. I have never forgotten that moment, but I forgot his name.

We prayed before meals especially if there was a preacher visiting. Have you ever wondered if prayer should be offered before anything is eaten? Or wait until the main course is served? While we are at it, do you know what the word "amen" means? All may eat now.

Unfortunately, in today's family life, people rarely dine at home or enjoy weekend activities together. Being on the farm was hard back then, but it gave us purpose and boundaries. We went to church every Sunday followed by a big family dinner. Those are happy memories.

There were few distractions from our core family mostly because money was tight. We grew up having every meal at home. When we did eat out, it usually involved times we were administering agriculture duties, like going to fairs, getting parts and supplies, going to the feed store, and errands like that.

Nowadays, we find ourselves embraced in a new situation not only for the American family but families around the world. When the coronavirus had the world on a global lockdown, we all stayed home and learned new ways to agree and get along. Our patience was tested. Some still stay home to eat and work, others have relented and gone back to old habits.

Family life is the highest focal point for training in every culture. All lives begin with the core family. Important values and virtues once were discussed at the dinner table, and I feel they are being discussed again.

Maybe the coronavirus was God's solution to, "Hey everybody, stay home and stop being so busy!" It is unfortunate, but rage, hate, and discord occasionally develop in societies because there's a void in family and spiritual closeness.

So, what is the answer? Sing "Do Lord!" And remember the summer intern who did what he could to survive on faith.

A Cold in Your Pocket

I have always preferred handkerchiefs to tissues when a pesky cold or sinus infection comes along. Cotton is always kinder to my precious nose than paper. While a youngster still at home, I would use my dad's hankies. After I married, I used my husband's handkerchiefs. When he left, I bought my own supply to have for the occasional runny nose.

In 2010, we found a large quantity of ladies' handkerchiefs when going through our Aunt Bessie's belongings upon her passing at age eighty-nine. The handkerchiefs were hand-stitched, home painted, crocheted, with lace edges all different in many colors and styles. They were almost too beautiful to use.

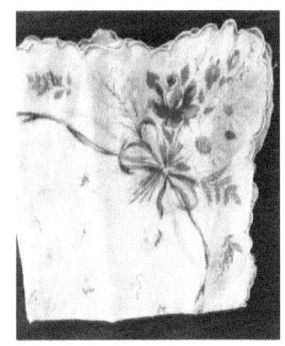
One of Aunt Bessie's handkerchiefs

By Christmas 2010, I researched the history of ladies' handkerchiefs and gave a printout of the research along with one of Aunt Bessie's very own handkerchiefs to each female of the Dow family. They were happy to receive the precious family heirloom.

Handkerchiefs originated in China about 1,000 BC. They were first used to shield their heads from the hot sun. The Romans waved hankies in the air at public games. In fact, the drop of a handkerchief signaled the start of a chariot race. In the Middle Ages, a knight would tie the hankie of his love to the back of his helmet for good luck in a fight. Renaissance portraits show both men and women with a handkerchief embroidered and edged in lace. Handkerchiefs even appeared in some of Shakespeare's plays. As far back as 1665, they were considered so valuable they appeared in dowries and bequeathed in wills.

In Persia (currently known as Iran, Iraq, etc.), they were a sign of nobility and reserved for kings. Hankies were included in portraits of the aristocrats. The more embellished the better, for the handkerchiefs indicated status and position. In 1785, the French King Louis XVI issued a decree prohibiting anyone from carrying a handkerchief larger than his. Seriously? What a narcissist.

Traditions tell of a bride borrowing a hankie for her wedding because hankies became too expensive. Often, hankies served as a medium for sending messages during courtship. This flirtatious endeavor continued well into the Victorian era. Even Queen Elizabeth I carried handkerchiefs embroidered in gold and silver threads.

During the hard times of the United States depression era, a handkerchief was often the only new item women could afford. She could "change" her wardrobe by changing her hankies. Soldiers, sailors, and airmen carried their loved ones' hankie during WWI and WWII. Many service men were issued handkerchiefs that were imprinted with maps. This showed the locations where they were fighting and bombing. If they were trapped behind enemy lines, the map in their pocket came in handy. Clever?

The birth of Kleenex was thought to be the death of the beloved handkerchief. Invented in the 1920s, by the 1930s the Kleenex slogan was, "Don't carry a cold in your pocket."

Mothers sent their school children with two handkerchiefs. The ritual of "show and blow" was the trend. Clever moms provided one hanky for children to blow their nose, and the other was a decorative one for show.

The Japanese women used the sleeves in their kimonos to store their hankies. The left sleeve was the "blow" hanky, and the right was the "show." It must have caught on as I remember many women with their hankies stuffed up their blouse sleeves. Some still do, only they use tissues.

Starting in the 1950s, many companies advertised on the face of handkerchiefs. Soon, they were used for campaigning for office. In fact, there was a photo of a handkerchief Martha Washington used to promote her husband George for President at the Continental Convention before there were any presidents. Pretty smart wife. No wonder he became our first President. He was smart enough to pick a good woman.

Many people are collectors of antique handkerchiefs. Who knew? I only knew I liked them for my illnesses. I used them in the hot sun to shield my neck and to wipe my brow. More recently, the bandanna type is tied around my suitcase handles for ease of recognition when I travel.

When I visited King David's tomb in Jerusalem, I remembered we had to cover our heads and many women used a hankie as a covering. A friend remembers as a child that her school lunches were fifteen cents per day or seventy-five cents a week. Her mother tied three quarters in a hankie for her to take to school.

I wonder what treasures others will find when going through my belongings. Perhaps, we all have loads of precious treasures worth millions of dollars. Probably not. One thing I know, we were grateful for our Aunt Bessie and that she was of the era of useful and pretty handkerchiefs.

Hucksters of Long Ago

Peddlers have been selling their wares from their trucks for centuries. It started out with horse- drawn carts or wagons when traders traveled from village to hamlet as early as biblical times. Over the years, traveling salesmen and hucksters became quite common. They brought the general store to people who lived far from town. After all, this started when most traveled on foot.

Unfortunately, the hucksters sometimes were known as swindlers or pushy snake oil salesmen. They filled the minds of gullible prospects with hype and hope. Itinerant medicine salesmen tried to sell miracle cures for just about any ailment. For a while they developed a suspicious reputation.

When my siblings, Clara, George, and Lois were young, they recalled the huckster who visited the farm. George claims, "Back in the 40s, there was a 'convenience store on wheels' that roamed the countryside to homes and farms. If I remember correctly, the truck was a converted school bus. The driver stopped alongside the road in front of each home. A family member, usually the wife, entered the vehicle shopping for necessities. They paid the huckster as they exited. Often, the driver was alone. Then the huckster moved on to the next home."

George added, "Mom selected a few items which usually included bread. The next stop after ours was always Aunt Bessie's house. I think the original owner of this huckster truck was

George Sink. Later, he sold it to Peely Stevens. For some reason, the *mixed-up* older siblings called the second owner George Peely even though that was not his name."

Lois said, "Is that the same guy that came around, and we spent what little money we had saved to buy powdered sugar donuts? Or maybe that was the Omar Bread man. I remember the Chesty Potato Chips man who traveled throughout rural Indiana as well." (Some people had a milkman; we had a cow.)

George continued, "One time when I was around four years old, I was with Mom on the huckster wagon. I took a package of gum. Mom didn't pay for it because she was unaware. When we got in the house, I started opening the gum. Mom asked, 'Where did you get that gum?' I said, 'From George Peely.' She chastised me and said, 'That's stealing, George, you should be ashamed.' Mom gave me a dollar with a note and told me go to Aunt Bessie's where the huckster wagon was parked to pay for the gum. As I began walking toward Aunt Bessie's, I felt so ashamed and embarrassed to face George Peely. I simply threw the dollar and note into the ditch along the road and went back home.

"When I got back home, Mom asked me, 'George did you pay George Peely for the gum?' I lied and answered, 'Yes.' 'Where's my change?' I lied again, 'He didn't give me any change.' Later that day, Mom asked Aunt Bessie, 'Did Little George give George Peely the money and a note?' Aunt Bessie told Mom, 'George never came.' I was found out. Mom asked me,

'What did you do with the money?' I confessed, 'I threw it in the ditch. Then I started crying about lying too.' Aunt Bessie had compassion on me and said, 'Let's go find the money.' She put me in a wheelbarrow and pushed me up the road while searching along the ditch for the money and note. As I recall, we never found either one."

"I remember the huckster truck, but I can't remember ever going inside," says Clara. "It was a grocery store on wheels." The rest of us don't remember the huckster or anything to do with it, but we like the story.

However, we all remember the Jewel Tea, Fuller Brush, W.T. Rawleigh, and Cloverine Salve traveling salesmen. I do remember the bread man very well. Once Mom didn't want to answer the door for the bread man. She and I hid behind the wood burning stove so he wouldn't see us. I am not sure why we didn't go to the bedroom and shut the door. Remember, the doors and windows were always open. People listened and peered into houses as they announced, "Bread Man, you who, anybody home?"

Currently, we still have the Schwan man making the rounds. When I lived and worked in Scottsburg, IN, a Schwan man visited the office. Since there were six of us, he placed a small freezer in our office. We ordered from him every couple of weeks. Our goal was not to eat all the ice cream before we took it home.

Yesterday's huckster delivery isn't that different from today's ability to order online or by phone. We have delivery and drive-through shopping. For food, there is Uber Eats, Door Dash, Grubhub, and many restaurants delivering for free. Merchants will always find creative ways to sell their goods. I hear of some who will come in your home and put the perishables in your refrigerator and freezers.

There have been many times I have ordered online at the grocery store and then picked the groceries up after they have been gathered for me. I really like not walking around the store. When I do, many other items "jump" into my cart. These days, I am happy to oversee my own groceries for now. Someday, I may sing a different song.

Do the Lights Still Glow?

During my young life on the farm along Turkeyneck Hill Road, we spent most of our time outdoors. It didn't matter what season of the year it was; we were not indoors much except at night.

Since I have been relating these stories, on the surface, it appears our farm life was a charming and fulfilling memory. Many people have said, "Oh, how I wished I could have lived your childhood, it seems so quaint and full of life." "Well, all that glitters is not gold," is my usual response.

For any farm to be successful, the farmer must have a deep and dying love for the hard life they endure. Sure, it teaches the whole family a lot about many aspects of farming, but that doesn't mean they all like it. Working in the dirt, with the livestock, and in general enjoying the fruits of nature is a good life. But just because we are born to it, doesn't mean we want it for ourselves. Our dad sure was smitten by the farm, as is my brother, Philip, his wife, and family.

However, who feeds America? The farmer! So, before you go thinking I am poo-pooing the attributes of the farmer, think again. My respect for them could not be higher. I am thankful for the education I earned by living and working on the farm. Lessons learned which most never had the opportunity to enjoy. All free to me, wow! Our family is blessed by farm life.

Anyway, living so far out in the country, when it gets dark at night, it is black dark. I mean unless there is a full moon or a clear sky full of brilliant stars illuminating the earth—it is dark. The definition of dark is the absence of light. So, when you hear the expression, "It was so dark you can't see your hand in front of your face," that is common way out in the country.

When the chores were all done, we followed the porch light aglow all the way to the door. In the summer, the light would attract every flying insect around. This was before the bug zappers, subsequently, there were crowds of moths and other night insects dancing in the brightness.

One evening, Philip and I were finishing chores in the block building where the farrowing sows and pigs were kept. Farrowing means "to birth pigs." We fed the mommas and babies and gave them water until their thirst was quenched. It was dark, and as we finished, I heard someone say my name. I asked Philip, "What do you want?" "I didn't say anything!" he replied. A few minutes passed, and the voice spoke again. No one was there. This time, Philip heard it, too. After we shut the doors, we darted off like "scared cats" for the house. We had no idea what to think.

Between the house and the block building was a four-foot high woven-wire fence. The glow of the porch light again was our beacon. Approaching the fence, we both hurdled it like we were track stars. Philip and I were teenagers at the time.

One of the best things we dreamed about were planes. Our home was in the flight path of the planes flying in and out of Weircook Airport in Indianapolis. That was its name back in the 50s and 60s. The planes were twin-engine or four-engine planes, not jets. Their low elevation allowed us to read the name on the planes. I wondered where they were going, where they had been, and was it as thrilling as I imagined. It was awesome to dream about taking a trip on a plane. At this time in my life, I didn't know anyone who had ever flown on a plane.

Old propeller passenger planes like the ones overhead

Late on a cloudless night in the clean air, we could see the glow of all the towns and cities around. Deep in my young mind, at first, I thought something was on fire. I asked my dad about the glow, and he said, "Phyllis, over there is Paragon, yonder is Martinsville, and that giant glowing light to the north-northeast direction is Indianapolis." I remember going to Indianapolis to the stockyards or to the state fair. I knew it was big but seemed so far away. To see those many cities glow in the dark was amazing to me. However, there are no lights but the moon and stars when you are deep in the country.

I am fortunate as an older adult to have flown a lot and even have traveled abroad. I ponder and reflect on all those dreams I had as a child. When my flights are during the dark hours of night, I see the glow of many cities from 30,000 feet in the air. It makes me question about my life on the farm as a young girl and I wonder, "Do the city lights still glow from the farm on Turkeyneck Hill?"

Clara and the Fall Foliage Drive

If you are from the Midwest, most people look forward to the exquisite splash the colors the autumn season delivers. A good frost is helpful for the brilliance to burst forth. When it does, there is no flora quite as beautiful. Personally, fall is my favorite season of the year. The air is cooler, the ground is solid, and being outdoors has much to offer. I not only enjoy the gorgeous foliage but love conversation around open fires and the aroma of burning leaves.

My oldest sister Clara resided in a Martinsville nursing home. As charming and comfortable as she found her abode, going out of the facility occasionally was always a pleasure. On a sunny and warm Saturday, I paid her a visit. I asked her what she wanted to do while I visited; play cards or go for a ride to see the foliage. Not wanting to appear eager, she said, "Whatever you want to do." I told her, "Clara, since you are confined, let's blow this joint!"

That was all she needed to hear; she was more than ready to go. Her personality was not pushy at this time in her life. She knew what a chore it could be to load and unload herself from the car and so forth.

The aide helped her into my car. I was not planning to stop or get her out of the car, so we didn't take the wheelchair nor the walker. We turned south onto Cramertown Loop Road leading to

Mahalasville Road. Clara was delighted to see where she and her family lived for ten years at the old John McDaniels property. Veering right, we cut up a road leading into the back side of the Morgan Monroe State Forest.

What a voluptuous and full-bodied forest lay before us. The many multicolored hardwood trees were picturesque, God's work of art. Many of the forestry roads were like tunnels with canopies hovering overhead as we made each turn. Several of the trees had turned gold and orange. In another couple of weeks, it will be peak season showing off the massive autumn hues especially after a hard freeze. The beauty of the fall is so immense, we just draw near it to blanket and immerse ourselves in it the best possible way. Fall foliage is God's gift to us every year.

As we snaked down the forestry roads, there was hardly any traffic, only a few motorcycles and cars. In popular Brown County, roads were most likely packed to a crawl. This state forest near Martinsville is closer and every bit as enjoyable.

Along the drive we approached a picnic area and shelter house. Facing us was a line of Volkswagens. They must have had a rally of vintage VW's as we saw every model driving along for about a mile. Their route was cutting through the state forest in their funky looking automobiles.

Clara remarked, "This reminds me of back in the early sixties when our kids were young. Frank (her deceased husband) and I packed a picnic, loaded up the kids, and took a drive. We'd get on an unfamiliar road to see where we would end. Along the way, we always found a perfect spot for our picnic. Those were great times when the kids were young." I could see Clara's little smile as her mind was full of reminiscence. It felt good I was able to share that memory with Clara to enjoy as we rode along the quiet backroads on this beautiful autumn day.

The road brought us to Liberty Church Road and the new Interstate 69 interchange. We drove over the new highway and took Godsey Road into Baker Township. Winding around the river bottoms, we recognized many homes and farms. We had cut through there many times in the past when leaving Paragon and heading to Bloomington.

Eventually, we came into Paragon from the south side. These roads were our childhood stomping grounds, and everything looked familiar. The only difference was Paragon was rundown instead of a thriving town like when we were children. Unfortunately, many small towns share that description.

I asked Clara, "Do you want to drive by our old home place up on Turkeyneck Hill?" She replied, "That would be a real treat. I haven't been by there in a long time."

As we moseyed past the old water tower at the edge of Paragon, I noticed it was the same tank that had been there for as long as I can remember. Many kids climbed to the tank and wrote their names on it, then sat up there for a while. Of course, it was usually in the middle of the night. I never did, I was afraid of heights.

At the entrance of the Dow farm, there is a historic sign. "This farm has been in the same family for over 100 years."

The 100-year Hoosier Homestead Farm sign.

River Friendly Farmer of Indiana

Clara had not seen that sign before and was impressed. Creeping through the barnyard in the car, I paused at each safety camera to wave hello to my brother and his sons. Soon, they would see the videos and get a chuckle.

We stopped by the home of our brother Philip and his wife Patty on Denny Hill Road. Patty came out to the car since Clara couldn't go in. She was glad to visit for a few minutes, but Philip was out running an errand.

After stopping at a restaurant in Paragon for a stromboli sandwich, I delivered Clara back to her *"Five Star Hotel,"* as she calls it.

It was an amazing day with Clara, and she truly loved our ride. It turned out to be the most perfect time for her, as that was the last time she visited those places before she passed. I miss her so bad; we all do. Clara was wise and very generous her whole life.

Proverbs 3:13-14 reads, "Blessed are those who find wisdom, those who gain understanding, for she is more profitable than silver and yields better returns than gold."

County, State Fairs, and

Vacations

Pigs and the County Fair

What a hoot! My buddy Carlos on TV news trying to "walk a pig" reporting from the Johnson County Fair. That took me back to the days when we showed hogs at the Morgan County fair. We lived for the fair. The county and state fairs were the highlights of our summer.

As each in the family reached age ten, we could join a 4-H club to anticipate and prepare for the upcoming fair. Our mom dressed all six of us alike. We wore red gingham short-sleeved shirts and new stiff blue jeans. One special year, I remember we were really decked out for the hog show. Our white shirts had "Dow's Durocs" in big red letters on the back of the shirt with a big red hog embroidered beneath. Above the left pocket was our name in red. Of course, we wore our new jeans. We felt proud. (Duroc is a breed of hog.)

Mom and Dad with a huge hog in the early 1950s

Showing our hogs was quite different from what we see today. Showmanship seems to be a lost art. We *showed* our "barrow or gilt" in a crouched position, keeping the hog between us and the judge. We never took our eyes off the judge; it was a serious stare of intent. The purpose was to *display* respect to the judge. If he was looking at your hog, you would show him the

best side. It is sad to see how that showmanship is almost extinct in today's arena. However, respect in general is a lost art.

Now, my non-farming friends might ask, "What

Garrett, Philip's grandson, showing his prize hog in 4-H

is a barrow or a gilt?" A barrow is a male hog who has lost his *family jewels* and is a non-producer. He is a much tamer hog now and easily mixes with his fellow male hogs. The barrow makes a thick and heavy hog for the market. Good bacon and ham, so to speak. I often thought of our penal system and how much better we might be with repeat offenders who are so full of testosterone. Maybe, we could relieve them of their angst and urges if we just treated them like the barrow? But that will never happen. Much too barbaric.

The sperm producing male hog is called a boar. Rhymes with bore. Boars are generally **not** very friendly with each other. There are not many boars on a farm, unless they are being raised to sell. The gilt is a female hog who has never had a litter of pigs. Once she has her first litter, she becomes a sow. Now, if you are ever called a *"sow,"* you will know what they mean. There is your lesson on animal husbandry for the day.

Lest I forget, showing your animals at the fairs and winning Grand Champion, or placing high, makes your farm operation good for producing livestock. The farmer will receive high dollars for breeding or selling the hogs. The fairs' original purpose was for agriculture. Currently, fairs still judge agriculture as well as many non-agriculture projects which can be measured. This is excellent for discovering the gifts of the 4-H club members, and the process builds character.

Meanwhile, as kids, we'd walk through the merchant's tent, which is now a building. Couldn't miss our yearly yardstick, map of Indiana, and fly swatter, which were free. The latest farm machinery was always fun to climb on, but now that is off limits. The projects for clothing, foods, textiles, trades, art, forestry, plus others were all displayed in the 4-H building. The chickens and rabbits were caged behind the food concession tents, although not a part of the concessions. Then off to the carnival we'd go to look at all the rides and games. Sometimes, I'd ask if I could swing the hammer to ring the bell or shoot baskets. I never won anything because I didn't pay.

Lemon shake-ups and pineapple whips were my favorites. The guy would yell, "Pineapple, pineapple, pineapple whip!" My sister Lois and her boyfriend would walk around the carnival with me tagging along. He would give me a quarter to "Go play in traffic." I took the hint and the quarter!

The county fair is a reunion for the county. In fact, that's where my brother Philip met his wife Patty. They married in 1965, and they are still working at the fair today. Going to the fair is all about community. However, you don't need to "Walk a pig" like Carlos to go. Enjoy the fair!

4-H Livestock Trends

The Morgan County Fair runs in full throttle and usually, it is well done. It requires many hands and countless hours to make it run like a well-oiled machine. Thank you to the many volunteers. Some take a week of vacation to help at the fair each year. That is fantastic to have so many have such commitment.

One year, I attended the Johnson County Fair to see the beef cattle show. In the barn there were very few beef cattle, yet a lot of dairy cows. I overheard some talk about other neighboring county fairs not having the numbers of beef nor swine in the 4-H club entries. Here at our Morgan County Fair, the number of cattle and hogs are very low. However, the number of sheep and goats is on the rise. I heard there are 500 or more goats entered in the various classes. That is a lot of goats.

My sister-in-law is Patty Dow. In our family, we call her the "goat" guru. She has an affinity for raising and being quite knowledgeable regarding goat herding. I asked her, "Why do you think there are so many goats (and sheep) entered in the fair as opposed to cattle and hogs?" She said, "They are easier to raise and take very little space." When I was in 4-H back in the late 50s and early 60s, I don't even remember seeing one goat at the fair. However, I did see some sheep.

Then I ran into Ronnie, a neighbor of the Dow farm, and asked him, "Why do you think the trend has shifted from fewer

large animals and larger numbers of the smaller ones?"
"Economics— it doesn't cost much to raise a goat compared to a
steer or a hog. Therefore, just about anyone can afford to raise a
goat," Ronnie replied. By the way, we all grew up with Ronnie
and to call him Ron just seems wrong.

So, I asked, "What is the market for goats?" We know the
market for beef and hogs is steak and bacon. The common folk do
not eat much goat meat. Ron indicated, "Many buyers purchase
goats and sheep to supply the influx of the Middle East
population who eat them. It is a religious food for them.
Middlemen come from surrounding areas to these sale barns, then
sell to buyers in Chicago and other big cities." He went on to say,
"Goat meat is the number one meat consumed in the world." I
will have to research that. I have eaten goat meat once at the state
fair, and that was enough.

Patty stated, "Several weeks ago, we took some goats to the
sale barn in Amity. We were able to get $3.00 a pound on hoof.
These goats were from 40-60 pounds each." I asked, "What will
the end consumer pay for the goat meat?" "They will pay as much
as $10 per pound. Many end users will do the butchering
themselves. These aren't pets, so it isn't a hard thing to do," she
said. Unfortunately, the 4-Her names their goats and sheep, but
they usually sell them at the end of the fair. Did you know that
"lamb-chops come from baby lambs? Don't you feel bad?"

I did some research online and found, "Indiana Agriculture in the Classroom—Barn Tours." There is a wealth of facts I will share now. The challenges faced by many herdsmen are high expenses and low market values. There are other challenges, but many local farmers cannot compete when maintaining a herd. If the producer is losing money, they can't stay in business.

Beef takes about two years to be fully grown. During that time, the calf consumes a whole lot of feed. When taking a steer to the market, it may weigh 1,000 pounds or more and about 45 percent is edible. The good news is 99 percent of the balance is used for other by-products. Who knew?

Indiana is home to over 800,000 head of beef cattle. Approximately 40 head is the average herd in the US. This does not consider the dairy cows. They are every bit as important to produce dairy products we consume each day. Just to be sure you know this; veal is baby cow the next time you want a "veal cutlet."

Swine is the proper name for pigs or hogs. Did you know the gestational period for pigs is three months, three weeks, and three days? Guess how long it takes to butcher a hog? Three hours. Not really, I just made that up.

This is a fact; the 3,000 Indiana Pork Producers contribute over $3 billion to Indiana's economy per year. Really? It was on the internet, so it must be true. There seems to be a theme of threes when talking about pork. No wonder we have a story about the three little pigs.

Though the livestock trends have changed, the 4-H fair is still a wholesome place for youngsters to learn and develop responsible habits. The 4-H clubs are so much more than the animals involved. So, get your children involved in a club and enjoy the fair!

Memories of The State Fair

My first memory of the Indiana State Fair was being in the Swine barn. Swine is the proper word for a pig. Dow's Durocs were proudly showing hogs at the State Fair donning the same outfits worn at the county fair.

Our Aunt Bessie loved being at the fairs with us. Since she lived in Indianapolis at the time, attending the State Fair was convenient. Aunt Bessie passed away on July 24, 2010, the day after her eighty-ninth birthday from an aortic aneurysm. A year flies by fast, perhaps she didn't want to face her nineties. Regardless, we all loved her, and we miss her.

Anyway, Aunt Bessie would take my hand and off we went! She took me everywhere I wanted, as I wasn't allowed to wander alone. She carried Dentine gum in her purse, and she gave all six of us a piece. Aunt Bessie Dow was a formidable aunt. She never had any children, so she thought of us as her own. I think she liked me the best, or so I imagined. Aunt Bessie whistled loudly if she wanted our attention in a crowd. I never did figure out how to whistle like that, but George and Philip could.

We all enjoyed walking through the Horse Barn to see the horses. The Clydesdale and the Black Percheron were massive along with many other draft horses. We had a team of horses on the farm named Prince and Bess. I never saw them as they were gone by the time I came along. We remember the Clydesdale horses from the Budweiser commercials and the team pulling a wagonload of beer. You have probably seen them in person or on TV and agree, they are big!

Draft horses by nature are calm, gentle, and not easily spooked. They can reach the height of twenty hands and weigh up to 3,000 pounds (1.5 tons). Percheron horses originate from France with the Clydesdale coming from Scotland. (Hmm, you'd think there would be some in the Outlander series?) It is recorded that a team of two Percheron draft horses pulled forty-five tons when harnessed to a load. That is where the term "horsepower" comes from, their enormous strength. Perhaps a bit of trivia you can use? Maybe not. As you know, draft horses have been replaced by tractors and other machines.

On the north side of the track, we visited the DNR building (Department of Natural Resources) and looked at snakes. Not sure why because I was afraid of snakes. On the farm, we *often* saw snakes on the county roads. I wondered, if we see snakes *often* on the roads, how many snakes are there per acre? We had over 400 acres. One more good reason to live in the city.

Still on the north side of the State Fair, the "old timers" farming exhibits were displayed. There, you can watch how they grind corn for cornmeal, harvest honey, watch them saw logs for lumber, and build things from the lumber and so forth. They even have a building with old tools and machinery. People dress in period clothing and are willing to demonstrate their wares and skills. I find it quite interesting.

Speaking of *old timers*, I was reminded of a story when my brother George was driving a shuttle for the State Fair several years ago. He was in his early sixties and felt spry enough. George was proud he did not hit people when they played chicken, or pretended they didn't even see him while driving. At night near the midway section, he drove only as fast as the "knowing" person in front of him walked. Best yet, he was proud that he could "hold it" for hours because, "Who waits on a shuttle driver to potty?" Most fair goers will catch the next shuttle or just walk.

One self-respecting day, George was at a shuttle stop. A guy about his age or a little older asked for directions. The guy began his inquiry with "Excuse me, *Old Timer*" and that is all George heard. *"Old Timer"* he thought? "Who is this guy speaking to, it couldn't be me!" George was looking around him for an old timer. *(They walk among us and forget to look in the mirror.)* Poor George, knowing him, he probably gave the guy the wrong directions on purpose. George can be a stinker at times.

Besides the county fair, the State Fair is a suitable place for a concert. One can be entertained by some of the biggest and best musicians and acts around. I hope you *go enjoy* all the fair has to offer. If nothing else, make a memory, you might write about it in the future!

Vacations and Fairs Once Again

If you haven't hit the roads for a vacation lately, you are among the few. Many people have gone on numerous short and long trips recently to make up for sheltering in place for the pandemic of 2020. I say get out and go as much as you can.

I don't remember going on a vacation when I was a young girl growing up on the farm. The closest thing to it was going to the county and state fairs. Yes, they were great events. The fond memories are cherished in our minds and hearts.

As you know, the Morgan County fair happens every year in late July. If I am not mistaken, the Indiana State Fair opens soon after. Whatever happened to the state fair being after *all* the county fairs have finished? If you ask me, it is a challenge to get the 4-H exhibits to the state fair on time. But what do I know, I'm not in charge.

In addition to attending the fairs, Dad and I went to Norfolk, Virginia, in the summer between my junior and senior years in high school. My sister Lois and her husband Dick asked us to join them and their first two children to visit our two brothers in the navy. It was a road trip long before the modern interstate highway system, it took a while.

The drive seemed long there and back, but I didn't mind. I had never been out of the state of Indiana before. The trip was a thrill for me as I found traveling quite interesting. One surprise—

I was underwhelmed with the "Great Smoky Mountains." In my geographically challenged mind, I thought they would look like the Rockies. However, I quickly learned to love the *bigger hills*. They were simply larger than the ones I was accustomed to in southern Indiana.

Summer of 1966, me holding Kris Angela with Dick holding Kirk in Virginia

This trip is fondly remembered as an experience of firsts. I saw the ocean; we toured navy ships—both a destroyer and an aircraft carrier. Our lodging was near the ocean and had a pool. Dad buddied up with men who were net-fishing from the beach. They fished all night and caught several. I remember one night we had a fishfry. Our palates were delighted eating the bounty of the catch. It was a very memorable vacation of firsts.

The current days of traveling have been pleasant. Recently, I was privileged to travel by car with a friend to Rapid City, South Dakota. That's the place where Mount Rushmore is with the presidents' faces carved on the mountain side. No, their behinds were not on the other side. We stopped at many points of interest coming and going.

The beauty of the United States is best viewed by a road trip or at least a train ride. However, we found staying in the larger cities became a challenge. Many hotels/motels were booked early.

Therefore, the asking price for one night became cost prohibitive. I think $300 per night in a Holiday Inn Express in Sioux Falls, SD, is excessive. We chose a smaller town for the night about ninety minutes away.

Philip with his wife Patty and baby Tami when he was in the Navy

While going through Moline, Illinois, I looked to see the highlights nearby. I noticed the Deere Run golf course in Moline as well as the John Deere HQ. Since I am a golfer, I figured we'd stop. Little did I know that the "John Deere Classic" TPC tournament was the weekend we stopped. We didn't see the course nor the pro shop. Therefore, I didn't get my souvenir golf ball for my collection. However, we saw the beautiful sprawling and wooded world headquarters of John Deere. It was magnificent. Whether you are a farmer or not, it is worth the trip.

Going through northern Illinois and the middle of Iowa was quite the agricultural awakening. The corn was the tallest I'd ever seen. It looked vibrant and healthy. So were the soybeans and other grains like the wheat fields. What astonished me was the size of the grain bins at the farms, they were gigantic. The farming operations were something like I had never seen. One would think this old farm girl would have witnessed these things before, but I had not.

Through the flat lands of South Dakota, the wheat fields were plentiful. Then the cattle farms with herds scattered over the gently rolling hills were breathtaking as we made our way west. I can see how the lyrics to "America, The Beautiful" must have been the inspiration by these sights.

Have you ever been to the "Corn Palace?" Well, it is a must see. What about the Wall Drugstore? It is more than a drug store, it is a tourist trap in Wall, South Dakota. Who knew? This place is crazy big and a bit cheeky. Along the road for many miles coming and going, road signs are plentiful. You can't miss it. Really, you can't.

On the way back we stopped in Dyersville, Iowa, to see the "Field of Dreams" where the movie was filmed. It still looked like it did back in 1989. However, they have a red souvenir barn. The corn field was tasseled out and made the perfect photo. Though it was a small venue, it will not disappoint.

There is much to share about my recent trip, but more tall tales will have to wait. I encourage all to get out and see our beautiful nation as much as you can—while you can.

Regardless, whether you are traveling or just going to the fair, have a good time and make worthwhile memories. There will come a time when memories are all you will have, so be sure to make some doozies.

Remembering

Our Loved Ones

Mourners and Escorts

July is a solemn month in our family especially for the *Big Six*. (Our affectionate name for my siblings and me.) In 1982, we lost our dad on July 18, our mom the 21 of 1991, and 2010, our beloved Aunt Bessie Dow on July 24. These were the most influential people in our lives. Thank God, we did not lose them during the same decade. Nevertheless, we rejoice when August 1 rolls around each year and no one else has departed.

One summer not long ago, our family attended a funeral visitation for a childhood friend. George attended the funeral the following day. It wasn't the deciding factor, but the little country church where the funeral was held had a reputation for having delicious funeral dinners. In George's mind, he was envisioning; fresh corn-on-the-cob, fresh sliced tomatoes, fresh green beans, black raspberry cobbler, and fresh peach pie. You know, summer's bounty is on display.

Later, I texted him and asked, "How was the service and did you enjoy the fruits of summer?" The only thing he hoped for was a peach pie, of which he had none. It was all gone by the time he got around to it. *(George has a habit of having long discussions and being last in line, or the last to leave an event.)*

However, while there, George was able to enjoy a hearty conversation with our distant relative, Lewis. During the conversation, Lewis commented, "I am getting so old, most of my friends and relatives are already gone. I told my wife, when I die, you may need to hire mourners." George assured him that if he were alive, he'd come to his funeral. Then, Lewis agreed he would return the favor if George died first.

George asked Lewis, "How is your cousin Frankie doing with his cancer?" Lewis related, "It was the strangest thing. He had declined so badly and basically lived in his recliner. One day, he asked his wife to open the window across the room. Frankie struggled to get up and made his way to the open window. Beaming with a smile on his face, he held his arms up like a child would reach up to be held. Suddenly, he fell backward and was gone. Evidently, a host of escorts were waiting to take him on to heaven."

Then George recalled a story of his friend, Cherry. She lost her husband Dan to cancer. Dan, Cherry, and their two young daughters retreated with Dan's parents while he was suffering during his last days. Dan's mother, father, and wife took turns sitting with him during the day. Dan was especially close to his maternal grandparents, and they had long since passed. One night, his mother was sitting with him. With a sense of urgency, Dan was stirring and said, "Mom, help me get up. I see Grandma and Grandpa are here." His mothered replied, "Son, just relax and let them come to you." That night, his wife Cherry sleeping next to him, heard him murmuring throughout the night. It seemed like he was conversing with his grandparents. She heard Dan softly repeat, "No—no—like they were coaxing him home." At early dawn, Cherry gently said to her beloved husband, "Honey, go on with your grandma and grandpa. The girls and I will be okay." Dan's reflection was one of peace and calm. With his grandparents' escort, at last, he suffered no more.

Another story shared by Lily, my sister-in-law. "My mother went to the Philippines to visit relatives several years ago. While there, Mamma became ill with pneumonia and was hospitalized. They called relatives in the states to say Momma was very sick and to please hurry over. My brother, Gene, reached out to the hospital to find out her true state of health." George called the hospital, "Speaking with the medical team, I found that my mother-in-law not only had pneumonia but liver cancer which had metastasized from severe lung cancer. She wasn't going to live much longer. Lily and several other family members flew to the Philippines to be with Momma."

When they arrived, Momma stood up, was overjoyed, and greeted everyone. Soon, she was back in bed and failing fast. Many left the room late in the day although Lily stayed with her mother. Shortly, Momma said, "Who are all those people?" Lily turned looking over the room and saw no one. She said, "What people, Momma?" Then her mother began smiling broadly while addressing the names of deceased loved ones and relatives. She reached out to them and then she was gone. Loving escorts came to take her across the threshold into heaven.

Sharing those stories caused George to say, "I truly hope when I die, I have an escort to heaven." I am nine years younger than my brother George, yet I said to him, "George, if I go first, I will come back for you." "And I will come for you, too, Phyllis!" he reassured me.

Love is boundless— even to the end.

Love is More Than a Word

Valentine's Day is coming around, and most everyone gets sentimental. Valentines are good reminders. Perhaps being grateful for our loved ones goes unnoticed otherwise. I sure hope not. Receiving a Valentine card is always welcome.

I believe the lyrics, "Love is just a word until someone comes along and gives it meaning." I also believe love at first sight is sweet when it happens. Love at first sight usually takes one by surprise, without warning or expectancy. Sometimes, it lasts forever; but time always tells.

To be *in love* requires a different attribute of self. Giving up a *me first* mentality takes a special kind of love. It is an honor to share a like-mindedness with another and should never be taken lightly.

There. You have my philosophy on love. Of course, I am single and cannot prove my theories, but I do observe life. Below I continue my observation.

Reflecting on marriage, I have ideas of success. The following is one definition of a successful marriage. It's one where you stay married, agree, or agree to disagree. This kind of union has common interests aligning with the same values. Success in marriage is defined as a nuptial with dying adoration between two people. To cherish another and to be cherished beholds honor. Whatever way a couple achieves longevity in marriage, I feel is to be commended. I may be off base, but this is one definition.

Our parents were divorced after twenty years, six children and two grandchildren. It was a sad day for all, but realistically, we saw it coming. Our Aunt Mary and Uncle Jim lost their twelve-year-old daughter to a tragic accident. Their marriage never fully recovered from their loss, and they divorced.

By and by, Mom met and married a divorced man named Bob. Likewise, Aunt Mary met and married a divorcee, Rusty. Of course, having two sets of children is a challenge for any second marriage. All four of them had children from a previous marriage. However, both marriages stood the test of time, and all remained faithful and in love until death.

Our mom and her sister Mary were the best of friends. They tried to see each other often. At times, they lived next to each other, vacationed, and spent retirement time together. The two of them were a riot jointly, more so than apart. They were the type who fed humor from one another and made life enjoyable for all who were nearby. I remember their laughter since my youth. It was always a joy to be in their presence.

During their second marriage, they had husbands who treasured the very thought of them. The men cherished their wives, and the sisters honored their husbands. Of course, there was heartache along the way, but their marital devotion and love never waned. I didn't realize it when I was young, but they were a model for us to follow.

Aunt Mary and Uncle Rusty holding hands

I was reminded of both couples when my Aunt Mary passed at age ninety-three. She fell and broke her hip in late September 2018. Complications set in, and she never recovered. As Aunt Mary's health declined, her husband Rusty stood faithfully at her bedside holding her hand. That act of love was his daily portion as he softly wept. Rusty watched as she peacefully slipped away on December 3, 2019. Their daughter-in-law thoughtfully snapped a photo of their hands. I affectionately call it, "The photo of love."

Our mother spent her last few years in a nursing home. Her husband Bob was there to feed her breakfast every morning and stayed until midafternoon. One of us daughters were there to feed Mom her dinner. Before we left for home, Bob returned to see her a few hours before bed. This was his daily routine. Mom had a man who cherished her in sickness and in health. We were pleased for her, and she felt his adoration.

At the very end, all her children gathered at the foot of her bed watching Mom labor for each breath, Bob remained at her side. Finally, the nurse shook her head **no**, she stated to Bob, "I'm sorry." Mom was gone. Bob faced us and said, "I'm sorry, kids, I did all I could do." Here this man just lost the love of his life, and his first concern was to her children. We all should love that deeply.

Yes, Bob was a special man, fully devoted to our mother. We were so thankful for his dedication and care. So many people in nursing homes are forgotten and die alone. Mom was married to Bob for thirty-two years; she passed away in July 1991 from COPD and complications of a stroke which happened in 1987.

Bob eventually moved to Ocala, Florida, with his son Ron. In 2002, I was in Florida and stopped by to visit him for a few hours. This was eleven years after her death. One thing remained; Bob spoke

The Big Six in 1991

of Mom as if she died yesterday. It was evident he still cherished her deeply. What a picture of love and affection.

Isn't that what we all want? A steadfast love *until death do us part?* Yes, it is. Did these two couples do everything right every time? No. But they fulfilled each other to the core of their souls. Being together was right for them. It took a second marriage to find true love full of depth. They gave up self to have more of each other in the name of *true love.*

Above all things, there is a powerful *love* which knows no bounds. That *love* is named Jesus. His love is the purest of all. And the best news? We all can achieve that level of love. All we need to do is ask and then stand in His presence.

Yes, Valentine's Day comes around each year. Try your best to drop them a line or text to let your loved ones know you are thinking of them, and yes, that you do care. The way to feel love is to give it away. Let your love shine bright now and every day. Then blessings will follow you for the rest of the days of your life.

Then There Were Five

She grew up in a home full of love for many years. Her appearance was nothing short of a miracle. The first grandchild of what was to become the formidable Dow family. The family was always filled with respect, but through unceasing prayer from our ancestors, we became an honorable and hardworking family.

Clara was born on March 12, 1939. Our beloved Aunt Bessie Dow was probably the happiest of all to have a niece attend her high school graduation.

Fourteen months later, Clara had a little brother, George. They were almost close enough to be twins. All their lives, they were close. As a little girl, Clara was afraid of just about everything and George was her hero; her mighty warrior to protect her from harm. The two of them remained close until she went to heaven. Her loving and protective brother George remained at her side and was the last to see her alive.

In two more years here came a little sister for George and Clara, baby Lois. The trio were   bonded like glue all their lives. Like a well-oiled machine, Mom birthed the other three of us about two years apart, Carol, Philip, and Phyllis. Dad called all of us his "trusty arrows" for his quiver.

As I have grown and reflected on the magnitude of our family, I realize how fortunate we all have been. Not many siblings have stayed as close as we have without parents and grandparents to be the adhesive. We are tight, and we thank God for our relationship.

Sure, we all know it is a blessing to have such love, honor, and respect for each other. When one of us is hurt, we all feel the pain. When one has a victory, it is like we all won. God blesses us in so many ways, the best demonstration is our "family."

Of all the siblings, I believe Clara had the hardest life. However, she just kept on going and looking for the bright side. She was our template for making life good when maybe it wasn't so good for her.

Clara had not had the best health as she aged from one decade to the next, but she pressed on.

She was happily married to Frank Allen for nearly forty-five years when he passed away in June 2003. They squabbled at each other, but it was just their way of communicating. Their love for each other was the real McCoy. He was an extraordinarily talented man, and he deeply loved Clara, it showed. She missed him horribly when he was gone.

Though Clara had four beautiful children of her own, she took time to care for me anytime I needed. Mom left when I was nine, and Clara stepped in to be my guiding light. Whatever would I have done? Who would I have become if she weren't the one willing to set me sailing in the right direction? Sure, the siblings remaining at home all looked after each other. But Clara was the one who swooped me up and protected me many times when I couldn't take care of myself.

I am forever grateful for the undying love all my siblings have constantly shown me during my growing up years. At times, I could be a bit of a brat. However, it was Clara's unyielding guidance and tenderness that kept me on the straight and narrow.

Clara had the flu in October 2017. On November 1, she was admitted to the hospital and never returned home. She spent sixty-six days in the hospital and then was a resident in a local nursing home until she breathed her last breath.

The five who remain.

Before Covid I asked her, "How do you like the nursing home?" "This is like a five-star hotel," she replied. "If I need anything, I push a button and they bring it to me. They cook my meals, and if I don't like it, they fix me something else. They provide games and entertainment. Best of all, I don't pay any bills! This is a great place to live."

These things I write with tearful expression since we gave Clara up when the heavenly angels came calling on Sunday, January 3, 2021. Have you ever been with anyone near the end of their life? It cuts like a double-edged sword, doesn't it? We don't wish them to leave, but the pain of watching is more difficult than one can imagine.

While talking with my neighbor Donna regarding some of the end suffering Clara endured, I told Donna, "It was tough to witness." She said, "As Clara labors to take leave of this world and experience heaven...it reminds us of the difficulty birthing into this life which we have all gone through." That jolted me. But at the end, Clara went very peacefully.

And now... who will we ask those challenging questions of days gone by? Who?

The *Big Six* sadly is now only five. Clara is still loved deeply and will always be sorely missed.

Mourning the Empty Chair

Are classes offered on how to properly mourn? Should the common man and woman be aware of such a thing? I don't think so. The worst mourning occurs when we lose a loved one. How does one prepare for such a loss? I am not sure.

In Ecclesiastes 3:1-2a, 4 it says, "There is a time for everything, a season for every activity under the heavens. A time to be born and a time to die... a time to weep and a time to laugh, a time to **mourn** and a time to dance."

Therefore, while going through any loss, it is common to mourn. God indicates in His scriptures that nothing lasts forever. We only have *a time* for this or that.

Basically, when we know something unpleasant is on the agenda, it's human nature to put it off. Often, that's how we handle the hard things of life, we procrastinate.

Having had a career in life, health, and accident insurance taught me many things about planning. After all, having insurance is planning. It is "risk protection" in many forms. That is the sole purpose and definition of insurance.

Before my license is periodically renewed, I must complete twenty-four credit hours of continued education in the field of insurance. These studies are about as exciting as watching a fourth-grade spring recital but is a duty which must be attended.

My interest piqued while reviewing these courses. Luckily, I learned many ways to protect my assets and my heirs. I schooled myself in the various methods used for life insurance, wills, trusts, as well as other end-of-life instruments like long term care insurance.

While pursuing these kinds of sales, I became acutely aware people in general are not open-minded to such information—nor the sales therein. It baffled me. However, I understood the problem. If I weren't in the business, I might not be interested, either. Nevertheless, the root cause for most rejections is denial. People simply don't want to think about such things until forced to do so.

Unfortunately, the only insurance that is guaranteed to be used is life insurance. Puzzling how many people do not have any. Right now, it is one of the few insurances where the proceeds are tax free. Please make sure to protect your loved ones who depend on you when you pass.

When ill-prepared people pass away, mourning is a gift that keeps on giving. It is hard enough to lose a loved one but is even more difficult when debts are left, and the care of dependent family members is in question. Where will that source of income for those needs come from?

Suffice it to say my sister Clara, who recently passed, was well prepared. I am proud of how well she took care of herself. She was an example of responsibility for all those near to her.

Furthermore, the many reasons for mourning encompass all types of loss. Besides the largest emotional loss of death, there is the loss due to divorce, the loss of a coveted job or career, and even retirement can put us into a tailspin.

Another reason to mourn is the loss of health which causes former abilities never to return. Times when you, a loved one, or a friend must relocate can be heartbreaking. Who knew the empty nest was going to gut-punch us as much as it did at the time? Yes, the reasons to mourn are varied and plentiful.

I was astonished by my sister's funeral procession from the funeral home in Martinsville to the cemetery in Paragon. It was amazing how every single car and truck we met along the way stopped at the side of the road to display honor and respect. Some truckers even got out of their trucks, removed their hats, and stood in reverence. The processional itself was over a mile along the highway. That show of respect alone kept a lump in all our throats throughout the ride.

So, how do we mourn, when, and how long? The short answer is, I don't know. The long answer is it is different for everyone in every situation. One thing I do know: "Do not be anxious about anything and we can do all things through Christ who gives us strength." Psalm 34:18 promises, "The Lord is near the brokenhearted."

Rest assured knowing when we have heartache and sorrow, it won't last forever regardless how forlorn we may feel.

By and by, the end will come soon enough. May it be that we all endeavor to live a good and full life; live it well enough to be missed when our chair sits empty.

The Bouncing Ball and Wyatt

Eventually, there will come a day when the ball stops bouncing. We consider living while we can still bounce a ball. When the end time comes, will we have it all done? Did we check off everything on our "to-do" list?

Almost thirty years, I sold insurance for a living. While waiting to speak with the nursing home administrator regarding insurance, we sat in the reception area of the nursing home. This area is a sitting room or lounge for the residents to rest or visit. As I spoke with my fellow agent concerning all the tasks on our to-do lists, she asked me, "Do you think we will ever get it all done?" As I pondered her question, I observed the residents humped over in their easy chairs and wheelchairs. I softly replied, "Carol, those people have it all done." Suddenly, we didn't mind our never-ending to-do list. Life is about perspective, isn't it?

Our life has an odometer. When we trade cars, usually we look at the odometer and think, "This old clunker won't be worth much if I don't trade soon, it's nearing the hundred-thousand-mile mark." So, we trade. Truthfully, many of our automobiles are built well enough that with proper maintenance and care, they'd last several hundred thousand miles. Many of us like to trade in cars and get a new warranty. Besides, it is a plausible reason to trade if we have the desire.

Some of us treat our bodies like we will someday trade it in for a new one this side of heaven. My mom always said, "If I knew I was going to live this long, I'd taken better care of myself." We overeat, drink too much, and in general, overindulge. We abuse our bodies with dangerous jobs and sports and a plethora of other maladies. Then we wonder why it is hard to get out of a chair or bed.

I truly admire the people who caution their steps by appropriate exercise and diet. So far, I haven't met very many to admire, but I just know they are out there somewhere.

Our life odometer is set at birth, or so it would seem. Just like an auto, we don't always know the last day. While we still have a choice, we need to move and move as much as we're able. In visiting a physical therapist, she said, "Motion is lotion." I guess I need to keep moving or lose the ability, and I sure don't want that.

My knees began to revolt as I aged. I had to have one knee replaced, the other a meniscus repaired. I was, in general, sitting around a lot, now I can move more. After all, I worked my body heavily while growing up on the farm. My jobs were always physical with the hay bales, the feed sacks, the fertilizer bags, the ensilage, and shoveling. Plus, we worked with the livestock. From an early age, my body was used abundantly. I was physically minded, and I rather enjoyed the work and being out on the farm.

While playing many sports, more miles were added to my body. After having my family of three awesome daughters, I played softball, tennis, racquetball, then golf, and now pickleball. So, I kept abusing my body for health and recreation. I believe our bodies were created for movement and not to be stationary. Perhaps, knowing when to slow down would have been wise.

And now, like most people in their seventh decade, I tucker out. For years, I have referred to two Bible verses to bolster me.

First is Isaiah 40:31 (NKJV) says, "…those who wait on the Lord shall renew their strength; they shall mount up with wings like eagles; They shall run and not grow weary; They shall walk and not faint."

Also, Hebrews 12:1b tells us, "…let us throw off everything that hinders and the sin that so easily entangles. And let us run with perseverance the race marked out for us."

Yes, we are all warriors in this human race. Someday, all our races will be over, and all our check lists will be marked off. Then what will you leave as your legacy? Is it not enough that we lived, lived well, and died? No, it is better we did something worthy of remembrance long in our absence. Are we achieving that objective? We will if we plan on it.

Most of us have children, and some have grandchildren and great-grandchildren. Some people do not have *any* descendants for many reasons. The ones who have offspring are often blessed beyond their deserving. I know I am.

Our cousin Wyatt was called "up yonder" last Friday. We were on our way to visit him again, but instead, we visited with his bereaving family. What a loving and beautiful family legacy he left behind. Although he had prepared them as best he could in so many ways, his departure still feels like a slamming door. Losing a loved one feels like that, doesn't it?

As youngsters, Wyatt and his brother Zane spent many summers on the Dow farm, and we genuinely enjoyed them both. Occasionally, they came during Christmas breaks. It was always a pleasure to have our city cousins come to the farm. It was a treat, they always made life fun and entertaining.

When the Dow family get together for Christmas or at other times, their families are always invited to join us. Our cousins' families add a special dimension to the Dow family, and we love them.

Our cousin Wyatt, and his wife Linda in 1969

Most of us strive toward the beauty of a life well lived and appreciated. That seems to be the perfect ideal. Nevertheless, as our beating heart stops, there comes a time when our ball ceases to bounce... whether our to-do list or bucket list is completed or not.

Thanksgiving Memories

Thanksgiving Homecomings

As a youngster on the Dow farm, I fondly remember our family gatherings on Thanksgiving Day. It was truly a time to give thanks. The best memories were when my three older sisters and Philip would come with their families to gather around the table. George was away in the navy but would phone home on the holidays.

Deer season is in full swing then, and some of the guys would go deer hunting in the morning. Of course, back in those days, I never saw even one deer on our property. They'd still go out before daybreak sitting and waiting in case one just happened to cross their path. I suppose they were eternal optimists. One year, they hunted behind Clara and Frank's home. Nephew Brant didn't hunt and never owned a gun, but he went with them. He had a club along with a five-gallon bucket to sit on while he smoked cigarettes in the woods. Of course, smoking was forbidden, but he puffed just the same, and the deer may have gotten a whiff of the tobacco aroma floating through the woods. Of course, there was some ridicule from the other men, especially the die-hard hunters. However, when they all came in for dinner, Brant saw as many deer as the others, none. So, the joke was on them.

There were a few times before Lois and Dick had children, they came to spend the night on the farm. Our furnace was a wood furnace, and it was always cold in the house each morning. It was common to see our breath until the house warmed up. Where they slept, I put a couple large quilts and wool blankets on their bed. When Lois got in bed and covered up, she could hardly move because of the weight. How quickly she forgot how cool it can be living in our cold farmhouse.

Whoever oversaw preparing the turkey and dressing had to

Dad and Aunt Bessie before dinner

rise predawn to prepare it for the oven. The turkey would begin roasting in the oven around 4:00 a.m. It was always a 25–30-pound turkey to feed the many who gathered. After a few hours, the sweet aroma wafted throughout the home, and before long, everyone was up. The men soon went outside either to hunt or feed the livestock, while the women made delicious preparations in the kitchen.

As the morning progressed, more relatives kept arriving. Like most families at Thanksgiving, food was the central theme. Additionally, we enjoyed getting together and seeing all the children. The children loved seeing their cousins and play ensued.

Each year, it seemed, another child was born. Our family grew from just Mom and Dad to their six children, then six spouses. After each marriage, eighteen grandchildren arrived in fifteen years. As of 2011, we had ninety-six in our family, and many have been added since then. See what happens when two people fall in love? They are blessings in abundance.

As for the Thanksgiving menu, we always stuffed oyster dressing inside the turkey. We also had other dressing to bake in a casserole dish. Our sister Clara made homemade noodles and yeast rolls. Aunt Bessie made the Waldorf (apple) salad. Sister Carol brought fresh peach pies and candied sweet potatoes. Sister Lois made her famous date nut breads, banana breads, and homemade cranberry sauce. Philip's wife Patty made delicious persimmon pudding with whipped cream. We all pitched in for the rest of the dinner, like the mashed potatoes and giblet gravy. The fresh frozen corn and peas from the garden were buttered perfectly. Someone also brought other pies— pecan, cherry, and pumpkin. Good 'ol Frank, Clara's husband, would bring homemade mincemeat pies. They were delicious. But I never quite knew what was in the filling. He told me it was meat from a

hog's head, but I'm not sure. Hog's head meat just doesn't sound appealing, but the mincemeat pie was delicious.

Dinner L-R Clara, Dick, Kirk, Lois, Carol, Jim, Dad

We stuffed ourselves until we were *food pregnant* and full of tryptophan. Turkey is full of the amino acid called L-tryptophan which our body does not produce. Of course, amino acids are building blocks of proteins. I also know that tryptophan is used to make niacin, a B vitamin important for digestion, skin, nerves, and serotonin. Serotonin is a brain chemical which creates a feeling of wellbeing and relaxation. Hence, besides being full, you are full of the good stuff which makes a body sleep. This could be your educational portion for the day.

My question is, "If turkey is so good for us, why don't we eat it every day?" Some people do. I will put it on my grocery list right now.

Dad, Dick, and Jim after dinner and the hunt.

Gone are the days of our big family gatherings around the table on the farm for the Thanksgiving feast. We have our own big families now. That is typical when the parents and grandparents pass. When we lose a generation, cycles of life change. However, we still remember the days of long ago. What a joy it is to gather with loved ones anytime we can but especially at Thanksgiving.

A day set aside to give thanks to the Lord for all the blessings we savor all year long.

Those were special days of years gone by, and quite frankly, I miss them and the loved ones who have gone before. We are blessed to have had those memories. Now here is your assignment, you and your family make a memory, eat until you are food pregnant, and give thanks. Who knows, you might even take a nap!

A Reason for Thanks in 2020

With Thanksgiving Day upon us, we ponder—whatever do we have to be thankful for? Many families will safely gather to feast, share love, give thanks, and be blessed. That's a start.

This year is unlike any other in our remembrance. Many have unpleasant memories of the huge change in our world because of coronavirus. Sure, the changes have been immense and have taken a toll on our jobs, income, travel, relationships, schooling, and numerous other activities. At times, the adjustments seem unbearable. However, we made it through.

Marching onward, we endeavor to overcome and rise to the occasion. That is what we do. We tell ourselves this coronavirus is not going to defeat us. Sometimes, we are totally overwhelmed with our new way of life. The problem is, it's not like a tornado, hurricane, or forest fire that only affects a small regional area. This virus engulfed the world.

Feeling the depth of these truths makes it difficult to proclaim the wonderous things we could be thankful for in 2020.

With that in mind, I want to help you discover things that are happening which are positive and worthy of thanks. We dare not grow "soft" because our creature comforts and modern conveniences which were once common— are now few or have completely disappeared, for now. No, we stand firm and find a new path.

One thing for certain is we had a gorgeous spring. The weather was beautiful. From my perspective, it was perfect. Why? Because my lovely yard was filled with colorful flowers and green grass as never before. Many yards were a "show place." Home projects and landscaping were at an all-time high because of the "shelter in place." More people were home and found the time to spruce up the place. I was very thankful of my yard in 2020.

Our summer was not scorching dry and hot as it has been in past years. That was good for the farmer. They were able to plant early, and the crops were well rooted by the time of the dry season. Having an effective growing season usually makes a good yield.

By the harvest time, the good weather continued, so the machines could drive in the fields. I imagine they had a prosperous yield this year as a result. I forecast they had a bumper crop. (A crop which has high yields.) Hopefully, farmers can store their grain adequately until the price is high enough to make better profits. This is another excellent reason to be thankful in 2020.

What about the leaves on the trees and bushes? My trees had the biggest and thickest leaves this year than any. It was great when the hot sun was piercing the sky shielding my home. Therefore, I saved on air-conditioning. Indeed, a reason to be thankful.

Then the frost came, and the fall colors of the trees were displayed in brilliant hues. Everywhere I drove, there were beautiful trees. The colors stayed magnificent for many weeks. Massive numbers of people took country "joy rides" to view the beautiful flora more this year than in the past. Yes, a reason for thanks.

The biggest evidence of proficient foliage this year besides the temperatures and moisture, are the leaves in my yard. I've had to clear out the leaves on three separate occasions. Usually, I only rake once. No, I am not so thankful about that.

All a gal needs to clean up the yard is a leaf blower, a rake, and an old large flat bedsheet. I blow the leaves into a pile, rake them on the sheet, pull the corners together, and drag them to the street. Luckily, I live in an area where the city sucks up the leaves once a week. (My tax dollars at work.) However, someone must get them piled at the curb.

The year 2020 has produced at least double the leaves than normal. Consequently, I believe I can be thankful for the healthy trees, the ability to pay my city taxes, and the strength to drag a sheet-full to the curb.

The best reason to be thankful is the promises of God. His promises are true and never waver. For example, in Psalm 119:105 (KJV) we read, "Thy word is a lamp unto my feet, and a light unto my path." That means when we put our faith in God and not self, he will guide us.

Psalm 119:50 tells us, "My comfort in my suffering is this: Your promise preserves my life."

In Acts 2:39 says, "The promises for you and your children and for all who are far off—for all whom the Lord our God will call."

Last, Hebrews 10:23 says, "Let us hold unswervingly to the hope we profess, for he who promised is faithful." Basically, we need to depend on God and not self. Especially in the year of our Lord, 2020.

If you are with loved ones this Thanksgiving, you are blessed. Hug them and tell them how much they mean to you. It might be your last chance to be thankful with them. One never knows when the last time will be the last time.

Christmas Memories

Christmas and the Cedar Tree

When visiting with my siblings lately, it amazes me we lived under the same roof as children. Their seasonal memories resemble those of Hallmark Christmas movies compared to mine. My memory was more like either *How the Grinch Who Stole Christmas* or *Ebeneezer Scrooge*. Of course, their unwelcome nick name for me was "baby or brat" as I was the last of the litter. So, what do they know?

Children are always filled with anticipation to see the Christmas tree lights in the living room. They know Santa Claus will soon be here. We were no different, even if we knew the truth about Santa. We were like most children by being filled with the "wonder of Christmas."

Unfortunately, with Dad's lack of urgency in cutting the tree and bringing it into the house, the more anxiety we felt. When he finally caved, it was never a pine tree. No, only cedar trees grew on our farm. You know, those ugly, prickly, and yet fragrant cedars, the Eastern Red Cedar? They grew randomly and were free. My dad liked free trees the best. "O' Tannenbaum, O' Tannenbaum, how lovely are thy branches!" Well, "it ain't necessarily so" when dear old Dad dragged our lovely Christmas tree to the house. Our cedar was sure to have a dead side which always faced the wall. The tree probably had mites, along with a bird nest or two. But what did we know? We were kids and always eager to decorate our tree.

But first, our dad crossed two boards and nailed them to the bottom of the trunk, so the tree would stand tall. Jar lids and folded cardboard propped up the tree stand attempting to make it straighter or at least not to wobble. Gaps between the branches needed filling, and most of the time it stood like the Leaning Tower of Pisa. However, we were proud of our tree.

Every year, we'd cut out a cardboard star covered with aluminum foil leaving a hole in the center for a white or clear light to adorn the top. Cedars were not sturdy pointed trees like pines, so the "star" lay limp somewhere higher than our eye level.

Although the tree was meant to be triangular, some years the greenest tree was round. I remember our lights were the kind which are outlawed now. The ones which catch fire so easily. We also had those bubble lights and old passed down ornaments from years long ago. Stringing popcorn for the tree with needle and thread was a tedious task. It seemed we ate more popcorn than was strung.

The icicles went on last to cover any imperfections. The tree glistened in the night when the house lights were off. We sat and gazed in wonder at the beauty of our glowing tree for it was special to us.

Clara's kids by
our Christmas
Cedar Tree

At Christmas, Clara remembers going to Aunt Lucy's home. At her piano, there was sheet music with the words to a song which spelled out Christmas. Clara recited it to us just the other day. The song title is "C-h-r-i-s-t-m-a-s." She also remembers Mom getting a doll for the three older girls to share. That had to be tough.

One year George recalls living in the little house up the road when Grandpa Charlie Dow received only a book for Christmas. He felt bad for Grandpa. George also remembers feeding the horses and cattle in the barns after the gifts were unwrapped. He felt sorry for them, too, so he gave them an extra scoop of corn, or oats, and more hay for Christmas. That reflects his good heart even as a young boy. During my days, the chores and feedings had to be done before we opened any gifts.

"One year, Mom 'found' a game Santa must have left behind the sewing machine," recalls Lois. She and Carol also got to share a child-size bake oven. Who knew those were even around then? One Christmas in the big house, Philip, age nine, received a race car wood-carving kit. He carved it with a sharp butcher knife. While he was "driving" the little race car on his hands and knees, he accidentally dragged his foot over the butcher knife and sliced his big toe.

It bled profusely! Luckily, it snowed that year. Mom filled the blue enamel dish pan full of snow, then placed his foot in the snow which caused the bleeding to stop. Philip still has a scar on his toe, but he doesn't have the race car.

Dad always knelt on his knees while passing out our presents, one person at a time. It was a joy to see who got what. My memory was getting a "Tiny Tears" doll one year, and it wet the bed.

Dad on his knees with the family gathered

On New Year's Day while watching the Rose Bowl Parade, we traditionally took the tree down. That cedar tree was extremely dry by then. All the needles flew off as it went out the door. What a mess that was to clean up.

Good times were had on the farm even with the sorry looking cedar Christmas tree. We made it lovable and enjoyed it even though it had a dead side. Our different memories are expected with our age difference which makes for a pleasant exchange of stories. Just because one doesn't remember a time or an event the same as you, we still enjoy the laughter together.

The "Big Six" Christmas

Like most families, ours has grown exponentially. We have growth spurts with each generation along with lulls every few years, then more growth. Currently, *The Big Six* is gaining more great-grands at the rate of three or more per year. (*The Big Six* is our term of endearment for my five siblings and me.)

It is hard to keep track of the total number of our extended family at times, but we try. As of Christmas 2019, we have 102 total including the in-laws, steps, and so forth. Just think, it started with two people.

About half of the whole family at Hopewell Presbyterian

Because of the growth, we have had to move to different venues for our Christmas gatherings. Now, we meet at the Martinsville Senior Center. With all the ones who live out of state and the ones working, we still managed to have about seventy people present every year. Each year, there are new babies and toddlers to get our attention. These little lives don't know it yet, but they are a part of a fun-loving group of relatives.

Two of the Big Six' were fortunate to have their entire families present at 2018's assembly. That is unusual and was fully enjoyed.

While having dinner during my first day in Europe in September, I noticed a white haired, white bearded hefty man with wire glasses at the table next to me. I made eye contact with my traveling friend, Marilyn, and nodded for her to look at him. She mouthed, "Oh my gosh." The dude looked like Santa as much as anyone ever did.

I couldn't resist. Looking at him, I said to him, "Shouldn't you be in the North Pole?" He replied, "Even Santa needs a vacation now and then!" His wife stated, "He plays Santa every year, and I even play Mrs. Claus, too!" From then on, we were friends. As it turned out, they lived near Cincinnati, but we had to go to Amsterdam to meet our new friends. How nice was that?

After my European tour, I spoke about Santa and Mrs. Claus with the Big Six. They wanted me to ask them to join our big Dow Christmas. Santa and Mrs. Claus happily agreed to honor us. A joyful time was had by all as everyone was photographed with Santa and Mrs. Claus.

The Big Six with Santa and Mrs. Claus

The children were totally enthralled with their presence. Some of the doubters were filled with wonder, so Santa took his time with those children. We appreciated his diligence of making it real for all who believed. We never had a Santa at our gathering before. I am happy to say that having our North Pole guests was a big hit.

In lieu of giving and exchanging gifts, we play bingo. The gifts are sometimes new, but most often, they are items from around our home we don't need anymore. When one gets a bingo, they go to the table and pick a prize. We used to wrap the prizes in Christmas paper, but not so much anymore.

The little ones really look forward to this game. After about forty-five minutes, the ones not playing get loud with their conversation. Then suddenly, everyone is at the prize table picking out bingo prizes. It is uncanny how many called bingo at the very end. Wink, Wink!

Like most families, these types of gatherings (as well as funerals) are the only time we see some of our relatives. Many bring the same food or specialty dish every year. We love watching the little ones grow and mature. It is a good year when we have lost no one to heaven's gate. This year was another extraordinary Dow Christmas. The Big Six were happy to see Santa and Mrs. Claus once again and relive the magic of the season.

However, we all know the reason for the season. It's the Christ child, Jesus. If it weren't for that babe in the manger, December 25 would be merely another day on the calendar. We happily celebrate our gatherings all month long for that one reason alone. Praise God for sending our Savior!

Now comes a new year of hope and renewal. Bring it on, we are always ready for the new year and the joys that spring eternal!

Christmas Miracles

Every year, if we pay close attention, we see Christmas miracles. Many have already occurred or perhaps are memories of days gone by. Hopefully, you can add your own Christmas miracles as you reminisce while reading the following.

Years ago, my sister Lois and I decided to go to our brothers for Christmas. Lois, her husband Dick along with their three kids and me with my three daughters drove to Florida. Our mom and her husband wintered in Saint Petersburg, Florida, near where George and his family lived. Our trip would be a wonderful Christmas memory for years to come. That was in 1983—and we're still looking back at the wonderful experience.

My twins, Katte and Kitte, were thirteen, and my younger daughter Jessica was eleven. Lois's oldest son Kirk was a freshman at Purdue, her daughter Kris was a high school senior, with youngest son Keith being a sophomore, both at Greenwood High School. We were all looking forward to the trip with great anticipation.

Lois and Dick had a red Ford Escort, while I had a gold Plymouth Horizon. Yes, we were living in high cotton, or so we thought. How we loaded nine people and their luggage in those two little cars is a mystery to me.

Lois's family and mine head to Florida

Our plan was to get south of Atlanta departing after school dismissal the first night. We did get south of Atlanta, and Kirk helped me drive. The three who were in the back of my car had zonked out while Kirk and I listened to the radio. He knew every song that played. I got so tickled at him—especially when Elvis sang, "Blue Christmas." When the backup singers went up and down the scale as a reply to Elvis singing, "I-I'll ha-have ah ah Blue Christmas, without you." Kirk let out the, "wooo hoo hoo woo hoo." Did he sing that? Oh yes, he did.

George lived near a canal and marina. The kids walked over to see the boats at the marina, and they were astonished at the number of people living on their boats. They had Christmas lights and decorations on their floating homes.

The next morning, it was unusually cold in Florida. The sprinkler systems went off and left frozen icicles covering the landscape. We northerners had a great laugh at that until we visited Busch Gardens and froze our tails off.

On the way home, we stopped in the mountains near Monteagle, Tennessee, to take photos of enormous icicles from the water running down the mountainside. The miracle was we got there and back in one piece.

A few years ago, my friend had her six-year-old grandson over for a visit. She has a nativity scene displayed in her home. His mother told him, "We celebrate Santa Christmas. Gigi celebrates Santa Christmas and Jesus Christmas." The grandson asked, "Gigi, why do you celebrate two Christmases?" She replied, "Because I believe with my whole heart that 'Jesus Christmas' should be celebrated." He is satisfied for now, but his miracle will prayerfully come true another time. The little grandson will ask again and someday be told the truth about Christmas. Bless his little inquisitive heart.

Going shopping is not my thing. I do it though because it must be done. My friend Daphna needed a friend to go with her to the north side of Indy. I went, and we shopped till we dropped.

Two days later, Daphna wanted to go to Edinburgh for *one* thing. It wasn't there. I told her we need to check at Kohls. It wasn't there. Next, we went to Meijer. It wasn't there— but I finally talked her into something as nice as a "dutch oven." Who doesn't need an *Insta Pot*? I led her to the self-checkout. Reluctantly, this was her first experience. I told Daphna, "Get used to it, self-checkout is here to stay, only we don't get a W-2 for working here."

You know with masks on, and off, a gal can lose an earring or two. I have. This night I wore a special pair of earrings. After loading the Insta Pot into the SUV, I rolled the cart to the corral. When removing my mask while returning to the car, I instantly noticed an earring was missing.

As I glanced at my clothes, the ground around the SUV, I stated to Daphna, "I've lost an earring!" Immediately, a man passed by and said, "Did you lose an earring?" "Yes, I have." He replied, "I saw one on the floor a couple of isles into Meijer. Come with me, I will show you." There it was — on the floor. He picked it up and handed it to me. I took my other earring out and showed him. Now, what were the chances? "Tony" was my Christmas miracle that night.

Nowadays, "Zoom" may be the miracle for your family gathering in 2020. Merry Christmas!

More Christmas Stories

Jesus' birth has the world spinning every December. In our rush to celebrate with friends and loved ones, often we forget to remember—it all started with that very first Christmas in a little town called Bethlehem.

In October 2017, I visited the birthplace of Jesus. Currently, the little town is quite a metropolis, but the nativity scene is preserved in its authentic humble presence. The adjacent valley is "The Shepherd's Field" where the shepherds kept watch over their sheep. It is totally easy to visualize the scripture readings after my visit.

The Shepherd's Field Valley is the area where David was born, also the valley of Ruth and Boaz. Amazing how God chose these shepherds to hear first from the angels. As the shepherds heard the news, though afraid, they said in Luke 2:15 *"Let's go...!"*

We live a different life now. However, the first Christmas *was* all about Jesus, and Jesus *was* our first gift. We must never forget His significance of December 25 every year.

Most of us experience joy by giving gifts to those we love. As we mature, we are not as interested in being on the receiving end. When we do receive a gift, it is as important to receive joyfully, showing the giver full appreciation for their efforts. Everyone has received gifts which are quite the question mark or worse.

My immediate family and I enjoy celebrating Christmas. One of my favorite gifts once was two boxes of Domino's sugar cubes. I saw those cubes on a cruise once and fell in love with them. Who knew? Sugar cubes used to be so common years ago.

In 1955, I remember our all-school Christmas program at the Paragon School. I was in the first grade and each grade sang a song. All six of the Dow kids (my siblings and I) were in the program. My first-grade class filed last, stood on the front row, and sang "Silent Night." The remainder of the entire school sang it with us. The event seemed so large for all pupils to be out on the gym floor, yet we were a small school. I can't imagine a public school today having all twelve grades on the gym floor for a Christmas program.

My siblings remembered making divinity and marshmallow peanut butter fudge. Then sharing with neighbors. Our dad always wanted figgy pudding, but we made it with dates. The day before Christmas, our dad brought in brown paper bags filled with oranges, tangerines, and apples. Smaller bags were filled with mixed nuts still in the shells and hard rock candies. The bags varied in size, and he always rolled down the tops of the paper bags and sat them around the cedar Christmas tree in the living room. We shut the lights off and just allowed the glow of the Christmas tree lights to illuminate the home. The awestruck farm kids just sat there and dreamed of tomorrow.

Our country church, Samaria Baptist, always had a Christmas program. Then we went caroling in the neighborhood to see those who didn't make it to church. A few times we were invited in their homes for hot cocoa. That was a delight.

My sisters remember while living in the big house, from the second floor, we could see the first floor through the large pass-through heat vents. So, they would keep watch to see if Santa had come yet on Christmas Eve. Chances are, they never saw Santa.

There were occasions when Mom got us gifts after Christmas. Then said, "Santa hid them behind the bed, and I now just found them." It didn't matter to us, it meant we received more gifts. Perhaps Mom was an "after Christmas" sale shopper?

Years ago, when my ex-husband, Mike, was about eight, his parents along with his little brother, Greg, went downtown Martinsville to go Christmas shopping. While his mother was otherwise distracted, his dad, little brother, and he shopped for "Mom." They were so proud to buy her a new lamp and rushed out to the car to put it in the trunk while she was busy. The three males were beaming with pride regarding their purchase. They knew she would be thrilled.

All went well until the drive home. Another driver pulled out in front of them causing his dad to brake and swerve severely. Mike screamed, "Dad, be careful, you're going to break the lamp." His dad acknowledged him but was quiet. All along, his mother heard the whole thing but never let on until after Christmas, she didn't want to spoil their surprise. We can't put a price tag on that kind of love.

The lamp still lives

When my granddaughter Maisy was about two or three, I got her a pre-formed plastic snow sled with four-inch sides. I stood it against the wall behind the Christmas tree. After we unwrapped all the other gifts, I asked," Maisy, can you check behind the tree? I think there is another gift back there." Maisy went back to search and brought it out full of excitement. When her dad asked her, "Maisy, what is it?" She proudly exclaimed, "It's a boat!"

I am sure you have many similar Christmas stories you could share from current times or from many years gone by. They are as wonderful now as they were then when repeated, maybe more so.

Regardless, my hope is you enjoy your Christmas the best way you can. As always, Merry Christmas!

The Christmas Spy

When the hustle and bustle of "Black Friday" shopping is in full swing, we welcome the onset of the Christmas season. Of course, I noticed many Christmas decorations were up well before Halloween. Their excuse was Thanksgiving was later this year. Forgive me, but I know a marketing ploy when I see one.

My three little girls truly loved our Christmases when they were kids. The wonder and the joy of sharing loving moments together on Christmas morning is special. Those few years with my own little girls are gone, but the memories remain. Happily, they have their own families. Now Christmas with grandchildren has a special joy all its own.

Maisy is my first grandchild. Of course, when she was born, my life began again with a buoyancy of freshness I had long forgotten. Everything seemed new with Maisy in mind. I fully expected several little bundles of joy. But for now, she is the prettiest, smartest, and funniest little girl I have ever known. Every grandparent thinks that—until the next one comes along. I am fortunate to have at least one grandchild.

My Maisy grew to be a precocious little girl. She has a mind of her own and knows how to get me wrapped around her finger. There were a few times she didn't get her way, and she let me know it. One time at age three, she came walking into the kitchen after I had told her no about something. She stood there stating emphatically, "Gaga, I'm not happy" as her folded arms made an upward and downward motion. Her sweet face reflected her displeasure, as well. Who knows what she wasn't happy about at that moment.

Friends of mine who were already grandparents told me about the thrill of having the "Elf on a Shelf" for their grandkids during the month of December. For those who do not know how that works, it's a spy for Santa Claus. The elf sits on a shelf in a different place every day to watch the children. Supposedly at night, the elf reports to the North Pole regarding the child's behavior, giving the naughty or nice report.

At Maisy's third Thanksgiving, I decided to give her the Elf on a Shelf. After dinner, David, her dad, read the elf story to her. In her little mind, she understood but was unsure about the idea. David placed the elf on my fireplace mantle in the living room.

The Christmas Spy

When the kitchen was all cleaned, my daughters and I were playing a game at the dining table adjacent to the living room and fireplace. Maisy was dressed in her pretty holiday dress and long stockings. She stood in front of the fireplace looking up at the elf. Maisy announced, "Gaga, I don't like that elf." I turned to her, and she repeated the statement, "I don't like that elf." I said, "Why not?" Maisy proceeded to walk over to the other side of the room never taking her eye off the elf, then to the other side and back around to another area of the room. She stared at the elf intently.

Then Maisy said, "Gaga, wherever I go, it keeps staring at me, and I don't like it!" I asked, "Maisy, what do you want me to do?" "Take it back," she emphatically replied. I said, "What, take it back? Who is going to report to Santa?" Her response was, "I don't care, Gaga. I don't like him looking at me!" My laughter was withheld because she meant business.

Like any good grandma (she calls me Gaga), I took the elf *off* the shelf. Maisy grabbed it and put it back in the box with the storybook. Maisy then took the box into my office, climbed up in my chair, sat it on my desk, and proceeded to tape strips of tape side by side around the three sides of the hinged box the elf came in. Maisy then brought me the box and said, "There, take it back!" I asked her, "Why did you put so much tape on the box?" "I didn't want that elf to get out" she retorted! So, I took it back and never attempted to have the elf again.

That was a few years ago. She is my only grandchild, and I still affectionately call her my "grand baby." She loves it when I do. The funny thing is, Maisy is now in college and still dislikes Elf on the Shelf. The impression must have been too real for her way back then.

The truth is, we must choose how we celebrate the birth of our Savior. It is okay if our children don't buy-in to the fantasies. The reality of the babe in the manger is the true significance of our Christmas celebration. May we always remember to share and cherish the love God has given by sending his son.

Other Holiday Fun

Spring Break

When I was a kid, I remember getting only Good Friday off prior to Easter. Later in older grades, I remember colleges had a week off for their spring break. In the fall, we got Thursday and Friday off for teacher's institute. All the teachers went to meetings to learn how to do their job better. However, those meetings were not mandatory, and few teachers went. So, the state switched it to a fall recess for two days.

As far as snow days go, it had to be a blizzard for us to miss any school. Of course, we loved having a snow day and played outside all day until we almost froze to death.

Nowadays, all school systems usually take one or two weeks break in the fall. Then break the week of Thanksgiving, two weeks at Christmas and New Years, and two weeks in the spring. Ah, to be a school kid or in education during current times. It is no wonder they start the school year at the end of July or first of August and end the first week of June.

As kids, we had twelve weeks off in the summer and somehow remembered what we learned the year before. Students of my era and before were able to get their diploma and even attend universities of higher learning. Amazingly now they need shorter summers because the students forget. Maybe— as the generations reproduce, their brains are a little foggy and can't remember as well as we do. I'm going with that explanation.

Looking at all other industries who do not "hold the presses, we need a break," one wonders how it can be? How can others who dutifully have stressful jobs manage to drag in day after day? Simple, they have no choice.

Most jobs offer two weeks of vacation starting the job and increase from there if offered. Now, let's talk about spring break. We use the rationalization that if other people are traveling, God knows we all need a break, too. People who do not have children in school—go on spring break. Retirees who don't work and can go on a trip anytime still—go on spring break. What is it about spring that warrants a break? I think for most, a break is needed to bask in the sun rays or at least get away from the winter doldrums.

The perfect spring break is one when it is colder than whiz and raining at home, and your destination is a perfect balmy and sunny seventy-eight degrees the whole week. Upon your return home, spring has sprung. The grass is green; trees, bushes, and flowers are all in bloom and the air is perfect. Utopia! Though it rarely happens that way, we can only hope.

When my girls were in their first year of college, during spring break, Katte went to St. Augustine to play tennis for Indiana State. My Purdue girl Kitte had her break the same week as Jessica, a high school junior. Not wanting to be left out, we drove to St. Petersburg, Florida, to visit my brother George who lived there. During the days, we visited friends who were staying on the beach while my brother and his wife went to work. What a deal! Free lodging in paradise.

At this time, I was so poor I couldn't pay attention. So, we drove to Florida and had my car to run around. Back then, no one flew except the extraordinarily rich. Mid-week, my car choked to a stop near the Don Cesar pink hotel on St. Pete beach. Being a wise and thoughtful young woman, I owned a AAA card. I called for a tow, and they took my car to a dealership. On the way, my

two girls and I rode in the cab of the tow truck. This was before each passenger needed a seatbelt, so I had one gal on my lap.

When I went back the next day, it required all the credit on my only two credit cards and nearly all my cash to pay the bill.

Kitte and Jessi outside the dealership while we wait for George

On the way home to Indiana, we had to be on the lookout for Shell Oil gas stations because that was the only card I had for gas. In fact, it was the only card I had with any credit left.

In those days, gas stations didn't have attached restaurants or small grocery stores. They did, however, have a few items like bread, bologna, chips, drinks, and of course, candy bars. We gassed up and got our food items at each pit stop. When we arrived home, I had less than ten dollars in my purse. Those were exciting times.

Now, people fly off to elaborate and exotic destinations for their spring breaks and the other breaks, as well. It sure puts pressure on their summer vacations, but they go, go, go.

Whatever your resources, my hope for each of you is to spend time with the ones you love and make a memory on any break you take a vacation.

Palm Sunday Celebrated

Because of the COVID-19 pandemic in 2020, the celebration of Palm Sunday at church was cancelled. Can you imagine? All over the entire world, there were no church services for Palm Sunday nor Easter. It is hard to envision, but we know the truth since we lived through the year of shutdowns.

Now, each church opens their doors more freely. Many people are beginning to feed their hunger for corporate worship and fellowship. One Sunday, the sermon at my church was from Psalm 95 indicating we are made for worshiping together.

Our reading from Psalm 95:1-2,6-7 tells us, "Come, let us sing for joy to the Lord; let us shout aloud to the Rock of our salvation. Let us come before him with thanksgiving and extol him with music and song... Come, let us bow down in worship, let us kneel before the Lord our Maker; for he is our God, and we are the people of his pasture, the flock under his care."

However, church attendance was lighter back during Covid with every other row being taped off. Our masks were on until we got to our seat. When the service was over, we got masked up to depart. With most folks having had their Covid vaccine and building natural antibodies, going to church is now a safe outing.

Amazingly, Facebook shows people on vacation in all sorts of venues. I encourage everyone to get back in the habit of filling their pew. Congregating together in worship is good for the soul.

As you may know, the Passover celebration starts on Saturday at sunset before Palm Sunday and goes on until Easter Sunday.

The Triumphal entry of Jesus is described in all four Gospels. In the gospel of John 12:12-13 (ESV) we read, "The next day the large crowd that had come to the feast heard that Jesus was coming to Jerusalem. So they took branches of palm trees and went out to meet him, crying out, 'Hosanna! Blessed is he who comes in the name of the Lord, even the King of Israel!'" Therefore, that Sunday is celebrated as Palm Sunday.

On his way to Jerusalem, Jesus asked two men to go ahead of him. "Go to the village ahead of you, and at once you will find a donkey tied there, with her colt by her. Untie them and bring them to me. If anyone says anything to you, say that the Lord needs them, and he will send them right away" (Matthew 21:2-3).

We have heard many stories of the donkey Jesus rode on his entry into Jerusalem. Primarily it was a colt which had never been ridden. Secondly, the Passover feasts were taking place, and the city was flooded with great crowds. Next, though Jesus is the greatest leader, teacher, and prophet, he came in humility and peace. He also wanted to appeal to the common man, then and now. So, he rode a donkey and not an impressive horse of other great leaders.

Additionally, I remember there was a donkey present at the manger when Jesus was born. I wasn't there, but that is what the scriptures tell us. Some readings say the donkey he rode on his triumphal entry into Jerusalem was present at Calvary where Jesus died on the cross.

Since then, the breed of donkey with a cross on its back reflects our Savior whom he carried into Jerusalem. To this day, that type of donkey still reflects the cross markings on their back. A beast of burden.

Between the triumphal entry and the crucifixion many events happened the last week of Jesus's life. He cursed the fig tree, cleared the temple, and he taught in the temple. He gathered with his disciples in the upper room for prayer and teaching them the sacraments of the last supper. Jesus retired to the Garden of Gethsemane to pray. That's where he was betrayed and arrested. His last week was remarkably busy.

Therefore, we call the week between Palm Sunday and Easter, "Holy Week." Hopefully more people will participate in activities of faith this year as they once did.

History tells how governments have taken over a country by first removing their freedom of religion and worship. Then they take over by disarming them and unfortunately causing the people to become dependent through entitlements. Before long, freedoms are gone, and regrettably, a socialist society is set. I pray that will never happen in our United States.

The Apostle John tells us, "If we walk in the light, as he is in the light, we have fellowship with one another, and the blood of Jesus his Son cleanses us from all sin" 1 John 1:7 (ESV).

With Palm Sunday on our horizon, let us all exercise our right to worship by supporting each other in attendance wherever we may worship.

There is a cleansing of the soul when we gather around the "beautiful river of God." Please go, become washed in the blood, and you'll be white as snow.

Easter Eggs

Which came first, the Easter egg or the Easter bunny? At this time of the year, some people have these sorts of questions. Do you?

Way back when, Easter eggs came from the Easter *bunny*. They were mythical creatures who delivered eggs to children in the seventeenth century by an "Osterhare," a German "egg laying" hare. This idea was apparently embraced in Langeland, Denmark, until the 1920s. As everyone knows—silly rabbits can't lay eggs.

In ancient Egypt, they discovered beautiful eggshells which were included in the tombs of prominent people. Most were ostrich eggs. They were still brightly decorated thousands of years later. Must have been the lack of oxygen that preserved their splendor.

Eggs are a treasured food. They are a pure form of protein and easy to prepare. Some folks avoid eggs because of the cholesterol content, but I believe that is a bunch of hooey. However, when those medical studies are written, I avoid them. If I don't know it, it won't hurt me, right?

Before industrialized farming, hens laid very few eggs during the dark winter. Egg production depends on light. So, wintertime egg laying becomes stagnant. At springtime, hens would once again begin laying eggs. The spring equinox is when the daylight is equal to darkness. This year it was March 20.

During the Dark Ages, eggs were highly valued. At that time, they used eggs as partial payment to pastors, servants, and for bartering.

Do you ever wonder why the grocery stores have an influx of eggs during the Easter season? Where did they suddenly come from? How do they get those chickens to produce more? How does that happen?

In all my research, I could not find clear and concise answers to these especially important questions. What I found was chicken farmers do their best to provide seventeen-eighteen hours of light each day for the laying hens. It is important for the hens to have good nutrition during their laying cycle and have plenty of calcium for the shells to form solidly. My imagination is they withheld shipment during Easter to industries who use egg products in their recipes.

Easter falls in the springtime when mother nature is groaning toward rebirth or new life. Flowers start to bloom, and baby animals are born. The geese are finding nests to sit on their eggs. Argh!

The church suggests the relevance of eggs during Easter to Jesus's resurrection. The tomb is represented by the hard shell of the egg. The baby chicks inside compared to Jesus.

We hear of "rolling" Easter eggs down the hill at the White House. I've never been there in person but like most, I have only viewed it on TV. That "rolling the eggs" symbolizes the stone being "rolled away" from Jesus's empty tomb.

When did we first start egg decoration? For thousands of years, bird eggs have been works of art in many civilizations. Emu and ostrich eggs were especially used because of their size and thickness. Some cultures used dyes, wax, scraping, etching, and even put on appliqués. These eggs made beautiful gifts. In some European countries, they use paper cut into flower and animal shapes and then applied to the eggshell.

The Faberge' egg replica I bought in 2019 while visiting

The Fabergé eggs are the most beautiful in my opinion. These eggs are created by Peter C. Fabergé originally for the Russian Tzar Alexander III. The first one was designed for the Tzars wife as an Easter gift. It was aptly named, "The Hen Egg." Easter is the most important holiday for the Russian Orthodox Church. Fabergé made fifty eggs for the Russian Royal family from 1885-1917.

When he made the first egg, Fabergé made the egg with a surprise inside. The surprise inside represented the empty tomb; that was a surprise. In this first egg, it was a piece of jewelry, and another opening usually held a tiny replica of the crown. Of the fifty eggs made by Fabergé for the Royals, forty-four eggs still survive. When traveling to Russia, one can get a replica of one of the Fabergé eggs.

The egg opened with the prize inside

As kids on the farm, we colored eggs with food coloring dropped into coffee cups along with some vinegar and hot water. We'd place newspapers all over the table and use spoons to dip our boiled eggs into the coloring. We had fun, but they were not beauties. In today's world, there are all sorts of ways to color or paint Easter eggs.

Philip and I dressed for Easter. George in the background

Whatever way you and your family celebrate our Risen Savior this Easter, rest assured, there will be Easter eggs involved. Some use egg whites for angel food cake. Then they use the yokes for egg noodles. My family's favorite is deviled eggs.

"He is risen. Yes, He is risen indeed!" Happy Easter!

A Mother's Day

Birthdays are special, and so is Mother's Day. Our mother, Dortha, has been gone since July 1991. However, we remember her birthday on April 30 every year. She did her best to be a great mother, but like all mothers, we sometimes fall short. The important thing to remember is we earnestly try.

I'm pretty sure there is not a guidebook or a course to teach mothers the myriad of skills required to raise a child. Of course, when I was raising my three girls, we had Dr. Spock. Although I didn't adhere to his teachings, I merely watched my older siblings raise their children and cherry-picked what I thought were the best methods they used.

Not a Mother's Day goes by I don't think of my mom. For a long time, I tried to reason what happened that caused her and my dad to split after twenty years of marriage. She didn't cease to be my mom whether she was present in the home or not. I was well cared for and loved by the ones closest to me. One promise I made— I would endeavor to be the best mom in the world to the three little cherubs who call me mom. Forever.

Of course, we all know of a few mothers who are not cut out for the job. And we know women who weren't privileged to bear children. Many would have made great mothers. In my opinion, those women make amazing Aunts. That sweet niece/nephew becomes the lemonade of their life.

This is from George: "When I was four years old, we attended a funeral. Afterward I ran crying to Mom. While ironing she asked, 'What's wrong George?' I said, 'I don't want to die.' Mom calmly said as she kept ironing, 'You're not going to die.' I thought, 'What a relief.'"

One summer after Mom left, she came to visit. Clara was driving and I was in the backseat of her station wagon with Clara's kids. Mom was riding shotgun (slang for the passenger side up front) and reached around to touch a grandchild who was sprawled out over my lap. As she looked at them, she took my hand and put a fifty-cent piece in it. Then she gently shook her head no as if for me not to say anything. Mom knew I never had any spending money, and she was barely making enough money to pay her bills. However, that little gift of attention was unforgettable to me.

All the grandkids were cherished by our mother. She doted on them in fun ways, and they loved it. We relished the times we could take them to see her or when she came to our homes. The grandkids loved her deeply, as well. My girls called her *Grandma Woodses*. She was married to Bob Woods, and they heard us say, "We are going to Grandma Woods' home." The *Woodses* just stuck, so we let it go.

One time, we stopped by her house shortly before her stroke in 1987. My youngest, Jessica, was fifteen and had a love for flamingos. Mom had pink plastic flamingos in her yard. After we got home, I saw one in our front flower bed. I found out later that Jessi took one and put it in our car.

Of course, I had Jessi phone her grandma to fess up. A month later we visited Mom at the Bloomington hospital because of her stroke. When Mom saw Jessi, she announced, "There's that little 'flamingo bandit,'" then she gave Jessi a hug and kiss.

Lois remembers, "Once as an adult, I was on a diet. I rewarded myself by losing weight. When I lost five pounds, I bought a new necklace. After losing ten pounds, I bought a new dress suit. One day, I drove into Mom's driveway in my new car. She asked, 'How much weight did you lose to get that?'"

My daughter Katte at twelve remembers seeing a photo of her with Grandma. Katte asked, "When did I get this photo with me and Grandma?" "That was me with my mom," I replied. Her Uncle George showed her a grade school photo of me he carried in his wallet. Again, she said, "When did I have this photo taken?" Katte was a mini-me back then.

When the first *Star Wars* movie was released, Buddy, George's son, asked Grandma if he could go see it. Mom never heard of the movie and didn't know the story. On the way home, Mom asked Buddy, "How did you like *Star Horse*?"

"I remember when we got a new Sears and Roebuck catalog," Carol recalls. "The girls sat together in the front room with Mom and looked at the new clothes. We got a dress or two for the new school year." I don't remember any of that, but I believe it.

Carol continued, "Our little home, up the road from the big

home, was on fire when the school bus dropped us off. Mom carried a big floor model TV out by herself. Later it took two men to put it in a truck. Mom must have been filled with adrenaline to have lifted it alone."

My mother and me in 1961

Yes, our mothers do awesome tasks for their families. Please honor them on their special days. One never knows when the last time will be the last time you see her.

Mothers and Others

Let's talk about mothers and the many things we adore about them. For example, how many mothers thought about or considered the day their child would leave home? I know it was a huge shock to me when my girls left for good. I somehow assumed they would always live with or near me.

The truth is, if we as parents do our job and do it right, they won't want to live with us. First, mine told me I had too many rules. Can you imagine that? Second, they needed their independence and freedom, mostly from me. They left, and it was better for them and still is; although, I love every moment we are near.

When my siblings and I graduated from high school, almost all of us "got out of dodge" as quick as possible. Two of us got married, two moved to the big city and started careers, and the two boys joined the navy. We all left the farm.

Our poor parents probably didn't see that coming. However, when brother Philip came home from the navy, he moved back to the farm and is still there today with his family. He is living the life our father always dreamed of for all his children.

For most, no one worries about you like your mother. When she's gone, the world seems unsafe, scary, and lonely. After all, what do mothers do? They protect, teach, and encourage; their first response is to spread their wings around their children. It's hard *not* to do that. Even when they are grown and on their own. No, we want to kiss their boo boos and rock them on our laps forever, don't we?

Surrogate mothers and fathers are a Godsend for many children. Those lovely angels come in the form of stepmoms and dads, older siblings, aunts and uncles, neighbors, and teachers, to name a few. Where would most of us be without their influence? Yes, they are part of the tribe, as it takes a village to raise children the way they should go. The adoptive and foster parents are a special breed of parents, as well.

Mom holding our cousin Donna, Aunt Mary, and little cousin Joan

Here are some fond memories of our mom. Sister Clara remembered, "Mom had a yard sale when she lived on Columbus Street in Martinsville. A lady came shopping and then put some items on the checkout table. She wanted to look around for more bargains, she insisted. 'Don't let anyone take my items.' Mom noticed the lady was the only customer at her sale. After the lady departed, Mom went in the house to laugh because she wondered 'who' would take her treasures?"

"I remember another time Mom had a porch and yard sale," recalls sister Lois. "The out-of-town daughters had a slumber party the night before at Mom's and giggled like little girls." Yes, those were fun days with our mother.

Good moments were had even during tough times. Our dad worked hard every day like all farmers do. Our mom kept us busy, made life fun, and did her best to keep us in line. She always looked for teachable moments.

Mom was her happiest when she and her sisters were together.

They were especially fond of one another as laughter filled the room during their visits. My sisters and I have good friendships, as well. We include the

Mom in the middle with her sister Martha and Mary in 1975

brothers in the frivolity as much as possible. As they age, our brothers have more time to go and do with the sisters.

Unfortunately, our mom and dad split shortly after the oldest child married and left home. That left five of us there to care for each other. It seems, we still persevere in that same mindset. I believe it is the moments during a struggle that define us; how we handle adversity is everything.

Some are amazed by how deeply we siblings love and support each other. I believe we all choose relationships over agreement which leads to peace when the battles of life rage.

Cohesiveness is more apt to occur during a crisis or at least some trauma when two or more are having likeminded experiences. We have certainly shared some trauma as well as drama over the years, even though we try to keep it quiet.

However, there is no perfect family. My friend Bill C. told me, "As you know, even the Walton's were only 'The Waltons' one day a week." But we all know their "John boy" turned out well, or so the story goes.

When Mother's Day Sunday appears each year, don't forget to honor your mother as best you can. For me, the best gift from my girls is to spend more time with them. I believe that's what we all desire as parents—more time with the offspring. The older we get, the more memories we wish to reminisce about our little cherubs and grand cherubs.

My mom told a story of a country preacher who came for Sunday dinner after church. This wasn't a true story of ours, but it could have been:

> As children, we were always taught to eat whatever was on our plate. One Sunday, the hostess served turnips as one of her delicious dishes. The preacher's little boy hated turnips—so he quickly gobbled them up first to get them off his plate. The hostess saw him and hurriedly scooped out more turnips as she said, "God bless his little heart, how he loves turnips."

Yes and—God bless all our mothers.

Farming During the 500 Race

When duty calls, most of us rise to the occasion. And if the ox is in the ditch, you get them out, right? In Luke 14:5 (NKJV) Jesus says, "'Which of you, having a donkey or an ox that has fallen into a pit, will not immediately pull him out on the Sabbath day?'"

The message Jesus taught the Pharisees indicated sometimes the rigid rules of the Sabbath needed to be overlooked if the situation was dire. I guess it is up to us to determine how *dire* the situation needs to be.

As young kids on the farm, planting corn on Memorial Day must have been dire. Our dad did the best he could, but often, neither the corn nor beans were planted before the Indy 500 race.

Throughout the previous weekends, we listened to the qualifications/time trials and picked our favorite drivers. Many people are big race fans. Though none of us had ever even visited the Indianapolis Motor Speedway as kids, we felt certain we were indeed *race fans*.

During the early years of the Indianapolis 500 race, it was on Memorial Day, May 30, regardless of what day of the week it fell. It wasn't until 1971, when the Uniform Holiday Act moved the holiday to the last Monday of May. From then on, they ran the race on Sunday, allowing Monday as a rain date.

Anyway, we'd go to the field early to plant on race day then come in for lunch. (Except it was called dinner back then. That's what country folk say.) While having dinner, the race started with all the fanfare and so forth. We hung on every word the announcer bellowed—"You are listening to the Greatest Spectacle in Racing!"

We were lucky to have a radio. Our imagination was in full color as we listened to the pre-race traditional songs and activities. Then Tony Hulman announced, "Gentlemen, start your engines." The roar of the engines sent chills of excitement coursing through our veins. One year, I discovered what all the fuss was about.

Back in the day, the race went on forever, or at least all afternoon. Well, it did because they drove 500 miles or 200 laps around an oval. Because of advanced technology, the cars kept going faster. If there were no wrecks, the duration of the race would be shortened. Rest assured, there is always a crash or two.

With a break in the action, Dad signaled for us to head back to the field. We hoped for rain in the worst way. Truthfully, we wished for a machinery failure, too. We just wanted to get back to the radio to hear if our hero was leading.

In 1966, as a junior in high school, I went to my first race with my boyfriend and his family. I remember that day like it happened yesterday. My sister Lois was enthusiastic for me because she had gone to a race a few years earlier. She felt my excitement and knew what was about to unfold. Lois accompanied me to J. C. Penney, a department store on the square in Martinsville. She purchased a new race outfit for me to wear on my big day. I was thankful, and we were both happy.

The Logan Bex family started going to the race around 1953 and made it a big deal. They lived for the race. Betty Bex rose early to fry the chicken. *(I had to get "rose" in here, as her middle name is Rose.)* She prepared a picnic, and we carried everything in coolers.

Our seats were on the bleachers inside the back stretch. I realized later those seats were a horrible vantage point, but I was in heaven. Without a doubt, I saw more than I could see from the farm. It was the most thrilling event I had ever experienced. I was attending the Indianapolis 500!

Aside from the fact I went in the wrong pit toilet (the men's) restroom on the back stretch, it was a terrific day. I remember the Englishman, Graham Hill, won the race. I wasn't a fan of his, but I have never forgotten his name; as the winner of my first Indianapolis 500 race.

My, how times have changed for the American farmer. The current high-tech tractors with their GPS and information technology make it almost automatic. The crops practically plant themselves. However, these days my brother Philip and his sons are usually the first to get their seed in the ground. So, they'd have no problem going to the race if they wanted.

Today's massive farm tractors provide enclosed cabs with heat and A/C. They're even equipped with radios. If desired, they could farm and listen to the race.

Yes, farming on race day is not like it was…back when my siblings and I were growing up. However, oddly enough, race day some years are still held May 30.

If you have never been to a race, it's a must see, even if you just visit the track and museum. You'll be glad you did because it is a beautiful sight to behold. Many people don't know this, but the Indianapolis Motor Speedway is the "proving ground" for all automobiles. Manufacturers are using the speedway for testing

year-round. If you are in the area, you can often hear the roar of the engines circling the track.

Have great Memorial Day

George and his daughters Michele and Loida

weekends, remember why we celebrate. It was first called, "Decoration Day," to pay tribute to US military personnel who died while serving in the United States Armed Forces. Please try to spend the holiday with people you love. The race is now aired on free TV in central Indiana. Enjoy it, and I hope your race car driver wins.

Memories of the 500

I am amazed by the number of people born and raised in Indiana who have never gone to the "Indianapolis 500." The "Greatest Spectacle in Racing" has put Indianapolis, Indiana, on the global map. For goodness' sake, please visit the Indianapolis Motor Speedway track and museum at least, you will be glad you did.

My first experience was in 1966. We sat along the inside of the back stretch. There's not much to see from that vantage point. But what did I know? At least I was there. Never having gone before, I bought my first matching short/top outfit for the special race. Englishman Graham Hill won that year.

The whole fanfare was more than this young farm girl had ever known. First there was a long parade with tons of celebrities. My favorite part of the parade was the Purdue marching band with the baton twirlers, the Golden Girl, and the Silver Twins.

This was back when Jim Nabors, a.k.a. Gomer Pyle, used to sing, "Back Home Again in Indiana," and Florence Henderson sang, "God Bless America." Next came the parade laps of all thirty-three cars rumbling and roaring around the track in perfect order. As the green flag fell, they immediately battled for the lead. In 1966, my ears felt they were exponentially louder than today's race cars. Nevertheless, adrenaline was coursing through my veins, and the hair stood up on my arms.

The food and drink at the race consisted of our picnic items. My future mother-in-law Betty rose with the roosters on race day to fry delicious chicken in cast iron skillets. It was her labor of love shown to her family. We enjoyed the chicken as well as other finger foods during the whole race. Foods were available at the concession stands, but ours was better.

Much of the day was spent people-watching. At seventeen, observing the massive alcohol consumption was foreign to me. Those race fans were hilarious to watch after baking in the sun and having too much to drink. Many were taking naps in the grass by the time the race ended. I thought that was a wasted ticket. Couldn't they have listened to it on the radio and slept at home? I was very naïve back then.

As children on Turkeyneck Hill, all my siblings remember well what we did on "Race Day." Normally, most people spend family time listening to the race on the radio. No-no, not ours. Not that the kids didn't want to celebrate the holiday. No, our dad needed to get the crops planted. Thus, we were often in the field on Race Day.

We remember all too well laboring to fill five-gallon buckets full of fertilizer and seed from the truck. The truck was parked at the end rows of the field where our job was keeping the planter filled when Dad stopped the tractor. During the later years, I remember taking the actual bags of fertilizer to the end of the row.

We knew about how many rounds he made before the next stop for a fill-up.

Often, when we went in for lunch, the radio was on. Hearing the *vroom* of the Indy cars, we knew the race was in progress. Occasionally, we didn't go back to the fields until the final lap. We'd wait until the winner drank the traditional bottle of milk which made the race officially over.

Some of the siblings remember having a radio on a blanket under the tall whispering pines in the front yard. They must have had a transistor radio because we didn't have an extension cord long enough to reach.

Since then, I've been to almost twenty races, and the crowd of 300,000 plus will surely change since the onset of coronavirus.

Kitte. Katte, Mike, Jessica

As you may know, the 2020 race was postponed until August. One can only imagine how hot it might be on an August race day. However, it can be a scorcher in May.

My girls began attending the race with their dad, Mike Bex, in 1980 and haven't missed a year since. It's become a family tradition that Mike's dad, Logan, started in the early 1950s.

Although the girls like the time they spend with their dad, when he stops going, they might stop, too.

Maisy and her friend

The Indy 500 always runs on Memorial Day weekend. As you know, Memorial Day is to remember any US military personnel who died while serving our country. It became a federal holiday in 1868, shortly after the Civil War.

When you gather this year, please begin new and positive memories to relay to the next generations of how you survived the COVID-19 pandemic. You will be glad you did.

2020 in the Rearview Mirror

Ah yes, the passing of another year. This isn't just any year of our lives. No, it is the hardest year most of us have ever known or ever will know.

We thought 9/11 was the worst thing that ever happened to us. 9/11 was a horrendous tragedy, but because of the worldwide nature of this pandemic, 2020 beats all. Frankly, *who* isn't ecstatic to say goodbye to 2020 and all the calamity this year has fraught? "Who" hasn't been affected by it personally, in your family, or close friends? A big fat "no one."

I have always tried to make the best of a bad situation. Likewise, many have done just that this year. However, unlike most disasters, no one, no country is spared enormous heartache and loss.

My friend Diane was scary sick. She lives alone and wasn't sure if it was Covid. Diane was so bad she couldn't get up or seek help. I texted her, and she responded she would reach out to me by morning. I prayed I would hear from her.

Throughout her prayerful night, she found peaceful rest. She awoke and texted, "I was singing the 'Battle Hymn of the Republic' out loud and felt the sickness had passed." Knowing Diane as I do, her singing surely ran it away. Thank God she did not have Covid. The lesson she advised, "Be extremely cautious yet keep on living. Above all, do not live in fear."

We all know fear is a liar. It can paralyze us and keep us from our best. Fear can be a heck of a rush when doing something dangerous. During those times, you've never felt more alive than when you are scared to death. Doing things like zip-lining, jumping out of a perfectly good airplane, or going through a haunted house. Those kinds of thrill-seeking fears are voluntary.

I had an involuntary fear of being afraid of the dark. After I was divorced in 1978, I left the outdoor lights and all the living area lights on every night. Finally, years later, I turned them off and prayed for God to protect me. Basically, I was just fed up with the fear. I have slept in the dark since.

The involuntary fears in 2020 are this coronavirus and the trickle-down effects. Millions have lost their lives, their jobs, their homes, their health insurance, and so many things we take for granted.

Strive to be at peace as we remember 2020. This pandemic year is over. It is old news, and we look forward to a new dawn and a new hope.

In Phil. 3:14 we read, "I press on toward the goal to win the prize for which God has called me heavenward..." You were not alone in the fight in 2020, and it wasn't easy.

John 14:27 tells us, "Peace I leave with you; my peace I give you...," Trusting Him gives you peace to handle your fight during a trauma.

In Romans 12:18 we read, "…as far as it depends on you, live at peace with everyone."

It is so hard to be kind when life is difficult. When we are thrust into a vacuum that we didn't ask for—we can get really mean. Try your best to be the first to show kindness.

Ralph Waldo Emerson said, "The purpose of life is not to be happy. It is to be useful, to be honorable, to be compassionate, to have it make a difference that you have lived and lived well." Don't we all want that for ourselves and others? Yes, we do.

During this time of "out with the old and in with the new," we must learn to put a period on it. The sentence is over, turn the page, and close the chapter. The book is finished and so is 2020! Hoorah!

Did you know that 30 percent of adult Americans live alone? Many didn't plan on it, but they are alone just the same. I don't mind being alone, I just don't want to be insignificant. In fact, when I go to heaven, I want it to be a real tragedy. Therefore, I've cancelled all my life insurance. Thus, I will always be remembered and significant. (Just kidding.)

When you list your goals for 2021, or any year for that matter, may they be ones you can keep. It is important to make goals and resolutions, but better yet to keep a couple. Try it.

Throughout 2020, one thing is for sure, Christ has not changed. He is still setting the captives free from their bondage.

My favorite verse is Jeremiah 29:11 (NIV): "For I know the plans I have for you, 'declares the Lord,' plans to prosper you and not to harm you, plans to give you a hope and a future." Amen?

We are all relieved that 2020 is in the rearview mirror. Continue to be strong and courageous and have a Happy New Year!

The big six in 1975
Seated: Philip, Clara, Lois
Standing: George, Phyllis, Carol

Me and my darlings in 2022
L-R Kitte, Mike, Phyllis, Jessica, Maisy, Katte, David

The end, for now.

Acknowledgments

First, I acknowledge the many family members with whom I have taken the liberty to tell our stories. But mostly I thank you for your love and support, not only now but all my life. Plus, I thank many friends who lent understanding and support as well.

My siblings by name:

Clara, even though you have already left this world, you were always my biggest cheerleader. When I started writing the columns, you showed them to everyone at the nursing home, and when I was there, you introduced me to others as, "This is my little sister, Phyllis, who writes those columns in the newspaper." You were so proud of me. Thank you for your tender love, care, and support. I miss you.

George, you make me laugh. You loved everything I did, and even if I got it wrong, you'd find humor in that too. Your stories were easy to write. It was and still is funny the way you say, "Hey, what about this story, you want to write this one?" Thank you for continually believing in me no matter what I've tried in life. I am glad we are friends too, *Jorgé*.

Lois, though we have been mates all our lives, I still try to prove myself to you no matter what. Mistakenly, I never thought you were proud of my writing until you had a TIA. The doctors gave you verbal tests for people who have strokes. The third time, you introduced me as, "That's my little sister, Phyllis, she's a writer!" You proclaimed that in your *altered state* with all the pride you could muster. At last, I felt approved! Thank you. I should never have doubted it because you have encouraged me throughout my life. I love you back, *Sissy*.

Carol, you have forever been so dear to me in all ways. Your respect and reassurance for me is beyond measure. I was your bratty little sister, and you loved me just the same. Your shy disposition was not understood until later. You were merely staying out of everyone's way and observing the family. That part of you has taught me patience and understanding. Thank you for your concern even now in adulthood. I always want to be like you. For example, I could use your home decoration tips. You are the Martha Stewart *do-it-yourselfer* in the family. Thank you for loving me dearly, but most of all, thanks for being you.

Philip, in our youth, you were my defender and protector in everything. You still look at me that way, and I know it. All my memories of you since the beginning have been awesome. Your kind and gentle spirit, to me, makes you a mountain of a man. Thank you for being a good role model for all. I'm grateful that you kept the farm. It is a legacy many do not have, and you have worked hard to keep the farm intact. The stories you tell about the past are amazing and sweet. Thanks for supporting me when people ask you, "Are you a brother to the gal who writes those Turkeyneck Hill stories?" Thanks, Philip *Ann*.

Acknowledgments

Debbie, you are the little sister I never had. It has been awesome to witness how you've developed and grown as a person over the years. You are the example of what perseverance and determination looks like when it comes to fruition. Debbie, we love you to the moon and back and not only because you are our golden niece *(the first grandchild)*. I hope you enjoy the stories.

My daughters:

Katte, Kitte, and Jessica, thank you for always putting up with my storytelling long before I ever wrote them for the newspaper. You three girls make my world better in boundless ways. I hope I don't embarrass you too much. I will try to put you in more stories, too. I love you more!

My only grandbaby:

Maisy Rose, thank you for showing your love to me— always at the right time. You are the best kid in the world. You are my favorite grandbaby, even though you left me for college. Seriously, Maisy, thank you for reading my stories and liking them. Hopefully, someday, you will know just how much I love you. I thank God every day I get to be a mother and especially a grandmother. Kisses and hugs.

My friends and comrades:

Georgiann, where would I be if I didn't have you to bounce ideas, readings, test runs, and you otherwise editing my work every time I sit down to write? Probably nowhere. Thanks for the help and support you have shown over the years. The many telephone calls when you listened to me struggle with words, grammar, and punctuation are so appreciated. You deserve more than a mention. I acknowledge you for all your continuous support. Thank you, G.

Lorraine, without you, I would never have been introduced to the editor of the newspaper. I would still be pecking away on the computer occasionally and not intentionally. Thank you, Dear. You are a wonderful person. Now get your story written and told.

The Heartland Christian Writers Group in Greenwood, IN. With Joyce as the leader, she always gave excellent critiques of my WIP (work-in-process) at our monthly meeting. In fact, the entire group is terrific at critiquing our *little darlings*. Thank you all sincerely for being so honest with your colored pens when you *slice and dice* my work. This has caused me to grow by leaps and bounds as a writer. We are all blessed because of our group.

Stephen Crane, the first editor who believed in me. I would be remiss if I did not fully acknowledge your superior influence over my writing. After all, you saw the author in me and gave me a shot to write a weekly column for the local newspaper. Thank you for your assistance. Your kindness is not overlooked.

Amy May, my second editor who requested my columns for the Johnson County's *Boomer Magazine,* thank you. This widened my audience to my backyard.

Also, to **Lisa, Eva, Linda B., Lou Ann, Diane, Cathi, Daphna, Donna, Marilyn,** and countless others. I acknowledge and thank you for all your support.

Mostly, **I acknowledge and recognize God.** Holding Jesus Christ as my Lord, Savior, Redeemer. Without His grace, I would not be the survivor and overcomer I've become. God has given me the gift of writing. My continuous goal is to use these talents for His Glory.

Credits

All photos are from the personal albums of the Dow family courtesy of:

George Dow

Lois Garris

Carol Teague

Philip and Patty Dow

Debbie Knerr

Katte Hanner

Kitte Allen

Jessica Bex

Molly Dow

Terri Dow

Linda Holesapple

Garnet Holesapple

About the Author

Phyllis Dow Bex has been a freelance writer for many years. Primarily, she has provided weekly newspaper columns in the town where she was raised. Phyllis has also written for her local newspaper offering articles and columns in a boomer-aged magazine.

Her lifelong search for learning has enabled her to express a wide range of interests from which to choose. Plus, her thirty-five plus years of selling insurance in a worksite marketing arena allowed her to meet all kinds of personalities. Phyllis quickly finds humor in most situations.

Now in her quiet retirement years, Phyllis writes. She also has time to travel, play golf, pickleball, and in general find enjoyment with the people she meets along the way.

Other books coming soon authored by Phyllis Dow Bex:

Tales from Turkeyneck Hill

Beyond Turkeyneck Hill